高等院校民航服务专业系列教材

民用航空实务英语
(第2版)

主　编　张　力　刘茗翀

副主编　杨桂芹　苗俊霞　车云月

清华大学出版社
北　京

内 容 简 介

本书共三个部分：第一部分为航班时刻表的英语表达法，以及城市、机场、航空公司、机型的英语表达法；第二部分主要训练机舱服务人员面对常规及特殊情况时运用英语的能力；第三部分为英语广播词，主要分为国内广播词、国际广播词、特殊情况广播词、紧急情况广播词和机场广播词等。本书专业名词均配有汉语注释，各单元均配有词汇表和练习，可供学生查阅和练习使用。

本书为民航服务专业本科英语教材，可供空中乘务等相关专业使用，同时可作为对航空英语感兴趣的读者的参考用书。

本书封面贴有清华大学出版社防伪标签，无标签者不得销售。
版权所有，侵权必究。举报：010-62782989，beiqinquan@tup.tsinghua.edu.cn。

图书在版编目(CIP)数据

民用航空实务英语/张力，刘茗翀主编. —2版. —北京：清华大学出版社，2020.4（2023.7重印）
高等院校民航服务专业系列教材
ISBN 978-7-302-54706-8

Ⅰ. ①民… Ⅱ. ①张… ②刘… Ⅲ. ①民用航空-英语-高等学校-教材 Ⅳ. ①F56

中国版本图书馆CIP数据核字(2019)第297776号

责任编辑：杨作梅
装帧设计：杨玉兰
责任校对：李玉茹
责任印制：杨 艳

出版发行：清华大学出版社
网　　址：http://www.tup.com.cn
地　　址：北京清华大学学研大厦A座　　邮　编：100084
社 总 机：010-83470000　　邮　购：010-62786544
投稿与读者服务：010-62776969，c-service@tup.tsinghua.edu.cn
质量反馈：010-62772015，zhiliang@tup.tsinghua.edu.cn
课件下载：http://www.tup.com.cn，010-62791865

印 装 者：三河市龙大印装有限公司
经　　销：全国新华书店
开　　本：185mm×260mm　　印　张：14　　字　数：340千字
版　　次：2016年3月第1版　2020年4月第2版　　印　次：2023年7月第4次印刷
定　　价：59.00元

产品编号：082701-01

高等院校民航服务专业系列教材编审委员会

主　　任：梁秀荣(中国航协飞行与乘务委员会高级顾问)

副 主 任：徐小博(北京东方通航教育科技有限公司总经理)

主任委员：周为民(原中国国际航空股份有限公司培训部教员、国家乘务技术职能鉴定考评员、国家级高级乘务员)

杨桂芹(原中国国际航空股份有限公司主任乘务长、国家级高级乘务员)

苗俊霞(原中国国际航空股份有限公司培训部教员、国家乘务技术职能鉴定考评员、国家级乘务技师)

刘茗舯(原中国国际航空股份有限公司乘务长、海南航空乘务训练中心教员、国家级高级乘务员)

高等院校民航服务专业系列教材
编写指导委员会

总策划：车云月

主　任：王　涛

副主任：李海东　姜琳丽　霍巧红

委　员：(排名不分先后)

　　　　周　贤　郭　卫　陈倩羽

　　　　徐颖丽　王瑞亮　郭　峰

　　　　姚庆海　李　杨　杨　峰

前　　言

　　2012年7月8日国务院发布了《国务院关于促进民航业发展的若干意见》，明确提出中国民航要"努力增强国际航空竞争力"，这是实施民航强国战略的重要任务之一。但就目前实际情况而言，我国航空公司在机制上还没有完全适应国际市场要求，国际化人才严重短缺。因此，只有培养合格的国际化民航服务人才，我国的航空公司才能成为能够提供全球化服务的国际航空公司，才能够增强国际竞争力和影响力，让世界听到中国的声音。

　　为提高民航专业高校的教学质量，弥补民航教材的不足，根据航空岗位的需求，提高民航从业人员的英语水平，"高等院校民航服务专业系列教材"编审委员会特编写了《民用航空实务英语》这本书。

　　《民用航空实务英语》(English for Civil Aviation: A Practical Course)是"高等院校民航服务专业系列教材"项目实践教材之一，可作为全日制普通高等学校本科学历教育空中乘务、民航服务管理(机场运营服务管理方向)、民航服务管理(民航销售方向)、民航旅游管理、民航物流管理、航空服务与管理等专业的民航实务英语教材。同时，本书可作为民航系统各下属单位的员工，如飞行员、空乘人员、空管人员、基地维修保养人员、行政管理人员等学习民航专业英语的教材和读物以及在职人员的英语口语培训教材。本书也可作为高等教育自学考试、成人高等教育、继续教育和广大航空爱好者的民航英语自学材料。

　　本书突出了以民航实务工作情境为主线的特色，体现了以语言交际功能为中心，多层次、全方位、多角度地为学生提供了最新的口语交际表达素材，题材涵盖了与民航业务相关的基本内容。

　　本书以最新的专门用途英语(English for Specific Purposes，ESP)教学理念作为理论依据，以学习为中心，把需求分析和教材评价作为前提，在选材过程中着重考虑教材的真实性、多样性、趣味性，在教材编写的每一个阶段都充分考虑到了民航专业学习者本身及其语言学习和未来工作的需要。教材设置的交际型任务不但能提高学生参与课堂活动的积极性，还能激发学生学习相关的专业知识，从而达到在真实的交际环境中完成交际任务的目的。

　　本书结合我国三大航空公司现用正常英语广播和非常规英语广播标准用语进行编写，并适当配有相应的中文广播用语。

　　本书部分材料由国航客舱服务部提供，在此表示感谢！

　　希望使用或阅读本书的各校师生不吝指教，帮助本书继续改进，使其能在高校民航外语教学中起到一定的作用。

编　者

Contents

Part I At an Airport

Unit 1 Introductions to a Flight Schedule(航班行程时刻表介绍) ... 2

1.1 24-hour System & 12-hour Clock Time ... 2
1.2 Airport/City Codes(机场代码与城市代码) ... 5
1.3 Airline Designator Codes(航空公司代码) ... 5
1.4 Aircraft Types(机型) ... 9
1.5 Business Class(公务舱) ... 10
Words and Expressions ... 11
Practice ... 12

Part II Conversations on Board

Unit 2 Service on Board(机上服务) ... 28

2.1 Greeting and Assisting to the Seat(登机引导) ... 28
2.2 Jackets or Coats(挂衣服) ... 28
2.3 Hot Towels(热毛巾) ... 28
2.4 Drinks(迎宾饮料) ... 28
2.5 Offering Pajamas, Slippers and Amenity Kits(提供休闲服、拖鞋、盥洗包) ... 29
2.6 Newspapers(送报纸) ... 29
2.7 Menu Introduction(介绍餐谱) ... 29
2.8 Drinks Offer(侍酒饮) ... 29
2.9 Clearing Glasses(收杯子) ... 30
2.10 If a Passenger Doesn't Like the Wine(如果旅客不喜欢这款酒) ... 30
2.11 Table Preparation(摆餐桌) ... 31
2.12 Meals(供餐) ... 31
2.13 Closure(开餐结束语) ... 31
2.14 Tray Collection(收餐盘) ... 31
2.15 Collection(整理餐桌) ... 31
2.16 In-flight Refreshments (点心服务) ... 32
2.17 Headsets(耳机) ... 32
2.18 Making the Bed(铺床) ... 32
2.19 Communication after the Rest(醒后沟通) ... 32
2.20 Offering CIQ Forms(提供 CIQ 表格) ... 32

Words and Expressions ... 33
Practice ... 34

Unit 3　Dealing with Special Situations(特殊情况处理) ... 44

3.1　Case Analysis: The Crew Seems to Be Ignoring Me! (个案分析：乘务员忽略我！) ... 44

3.2　Case Analysis: I Can't Sit by My Colleague! (个案分析：我不能和同事坐在一起！) ... 47

3.3　Case Analysis: The Service on This Flight Is Terrible! (个案分析：这个飞机上的服务太糟糕了！) ... 47

Words and Expressions ... 48
Practice ... 49

Unit 4　Communication with Passengers(与乘客沟通) ... 51

4.1　Boarding(登机) ... 51
 4.1.1　Greetings(欢迎) ... 51
 4.1.2　Seating(座位) ... 52
 4.1.3　Belongings(随身物品) ... 53

Words and Expressions ... 54

4.2　Before Take-off(起飞前) ... 55
 4.2.1　Safety Check(安全检查) ... 55
 4.2.2　Cabin Getting Ready(客舱准备) ... 56

Words and Expressions ... 56

4.3　In-flight Service(空中服务) ... 56
 4.3.1　General(常规的) ... 56
 4.3.2　Safety(安全) ... 58
 4.3.3　Beverages(饮料) ... 58
 4.3.4　Meals(供餐) ... 60
 4.3.5　Duty Free Sales(免税品销售) ... 63
 4.3.6　Phoenix Miles and Change for Hope(知音卡和零钱捐赠) ... 64
 4.3.7　Air Bar(空中酒廊) ... 65
 4.3.8　CIQ(海关移民局检疫) ... 65
 4.3.9　Relaxation(娱乐休息) ... 66

Words and Expressions ... 68

4.4　Landing(落地) ... 70
 4.4.1　Disembarkation(下客) ... 70
 4.4.2　Airport and Destination(机场和目的地) ... 71
 4.4.3　China Beijing(中国北京) ... 72
 4.4.4　Airport Service(机场服务) ... 73

Words and Expressions ... 74

4.5　Special Situations(特殊情况) ... 75
 4.5.1　Explanation and Service(安抚) ... 75

	4.5.2	Disembarkation(下客)	76
	4.5.3	Complaint(投诉)	76
	4.5.4	Lost & Found(失物认领)	78

4.6 Special Passengers(特殊旅客) 78
    4.6.1 UM(无人陪伴儿童) 78
    4.6.2 CIP(常旅客) 79
    4.6.3 Disabled Passengers(残疾旅客) 79
    4.6.4 Infants(婴儿) 81
    4.6.5 Sickness(不适或疾病) 81

4.7 Emergency Situation(紧急情况) 82

Words and Expressions 82

Practice 83

Part Ⅲ Announcements

Unit 5 Domestic Cabin Announcements(国内机舱广播) 106

5.1 Prior to Take-off(起飞前) 106
    5.1.1 Welcome(欢迎词) 106
    5.1.2 Safety Demonstration(安全演示) 107
    5.1.3 Seat Belt Confirmation Prior to Take-off (起飞前确认系好安全带) 108
    5.1.4 Domestic Order of Service(国内航线及服务介绍) 108

Words and Expressions 109

5.2 Prior to Landing(着陆前) 110
    5.2.1 Before Landing(着陆前) 110
    5.2.2 Farewell and Giving Regards(着陆前致意) 111
    5.2.3 Video Demonstration of the Transit Procedures(中转流程的视频演示) 111
    5.2.4 Announcement of Transit Flights(中转航班通告) 112
    5.2.5 Seat Belt Confirmation Before Landing(落地前确认系好安全带) 112
    5.2.6 Transit(中途着陆) 112
    5.2.7 Terminal Landing(终点着陆) 113

Words and Expressions 114

Practice 115

Unit 6 International Cabin Announcements(国际机舱广播) 122

6.1 Prior to Take-off(起飞前) 122
    6.1.1 Welcome(欢迎词) 122
    6.1.2 Safety Demonstration(安全演示) 123
    6.1.3 Seat Belt Confirmation Prior to Take-off(起飞前确认系好安全带) 124
    6.1.4 International Order of Service(国际航线及服务介绍) 125

	6.1.5	Quarantine (General)[检疫规定(通用)]	126
	6.1.6	Quarantine in Italy(意大利检疫规定)	126
	6.1.7	Quarantine in Australia(澳大利亚检疫规定)	127
	6.1.8	Quarantine in Japan(日本检疫规定)	127
	6.1.9	Entry Documents and Immigration Regulations(入境及海关规定)	128
	6.1.10	Completion of Landing Forms(美国申报单填写)	128
	6.1.11	Japanese Immigration Regulations(日本入境规定)	129
	6.1.12	German Immigration Regulations(德国入境规定)	129

Words and Expressions 130

6.2 During Flight(飞行期间) 130
    6.2.1 Cruising(平稳航行中) 130
    6.2.2 Duty-free Sales(出售免税品广播) 131
    6.2.3 Health Video(健康养生视频) 132
    6.2.4 Concluding the Duty-free Sales(停止出售免税品广播) 132
    6.2.5 Spraying for Disinfection(喷药) 132
    6.2.6 20/30 Minutes Prior to Landing(着陆前 20/30 分钟) 133
    6.2.7 Farewell and Giving Regards(着陆前致意) 134
    6.2.8 Video Demonstration of the Transit Procedures(视频演示中转流程) 134
    6.2.9 Announcement of Transit Flights(中转航班通告) 134

Words and Expressions 135

6.3 Prior to Landing(落地前) 136
    6.3.1 Seat Belt Fastened(确认系好安全带) 136
    6.3.2 Terminal Landing(终点着陆) 136
    6.3.3 International-domestic Connecting(国内经停) 137
    6.3.4 International Connecting(国际经停) 139
    6.3.5 International Connecting-PAX(国际经停，旅客机上等候) 140

Words and Expressions 141
Practice 141

Unit 7　Special Occasions Announcements(特殊情况广播) 152

7.1 Brief Introduction(简要介绍) 152
    7.1.1 Organizations(各类团体) 152
    7.1.2 Maiden Flight(首航) 152
    7.1.3 Anniversary of Air China(中国国际航空周年纪念日) 153
    7.1.4 Merged Flights(合并航班) 153
    7.1.5 Take-off(中途起飞) 154

Words and Expressions 155

7.2 In the Cabin(舱内情况) 155
    7.2.1 Prior to Door Closing(关舱门登机前) 155

7.2.2	Picking up Duty-free Merchandise(领取免税品)	155
7.2.3	Head Count(清点旅客)	156
7.2.4	Passengers Cancel Journey(因旅客临时取消航班而清舱)	156
7.2.5	Temporarily Adjusting Seats(临时调整座位)	157
7.2.6	Auxiliary Power Supply Failure and Increase of CabinTemperature(APU 故障，客舱温度过高)	157
7.2.7	Delay in Departure(延误起飞)	158
7.2.8	Delay (Congestion)[延误(飞机排队等待起飞)]	158
7.2.9	Extended Delay(继续延误)	158
7.2.10	Having All Passengers Rest and Wait in the Terminal(回候机室休息)	159
7.2.11	Changing Aircraft(换乘飞机)	159
7.2.12	Cancelled Flight(航班取消)	159
7.2.13	Safety Check(安全检查)	160
7.2.14	Taxiing(滑行)	160
7.2.15	Cabin Installations(客舱设备介绍)	160
7.2.16	Equipped with Telephone(卫星电话)	161
7.2.17	Immigration Form/Customs Form/Quarantine Regulations Form Unavailable on Board (机上未配备目的地入境卡、海关申报单、检疫申明卡)	161
7.2.18	Video System Failure(视频系统故障)	162
7.2.19	Clogged Toilet(卫生间故障)	162

Words and Expressions ... 162

7.3 Before Disembarkation(下机前) ... 163

7.3.1	Water Supply System Failure(供水系统故障停止供应热饮)	163
7.3.2	Lost and Found(失物认领)	164
7.3.3	Request for Medical Assistance(找医生)	164
7.3.4	Suspension of Hot Drink Service Due to Turbulence(因颠簸，暂停提供热饮)	164
7.3.5	Turbulence (Suspension of Cabin Service)[颠簸(暂停服务)]	165
7.3.6	Headsets Collection(回收耳机)	165
7.3.7	Flying Directly(直飞)	165
7.3.8	Circling(空中盘旋)	166
7.3.9	Landing Delay(着陆延迟)	166
7.3.10	Landing in Advance(提前着陆)	166
7.3.11	Return/Alternate Flight(返航/备降)	167
7.3.12	Returning to Airports/Arriving in Alternate Airports(到达返航/备降机场)	167
7.3.13	PAX May Leave Belongings on Board(行李不拿下飞机)	168
7.3.14	Taxiing After Landing(着陆后滑行)	168
7.3.15	Delay (Parking Area)[等待(停机位)]	168
7.3.16	Tail Support(货物太重加支尾撑杆)	169
7.3.17	Delay (Transit Bus)[等待(摆渡车)]	169

- 7.3.18 Taking the Transit Bus(停靠远机位，乘坐摆渡车) 169
- 7.3.19 Waiting for Inspecting Officer(联检单位未到) 170
- 7.3.20 Announcement of Disembarkation(下机通告) 170
- 7.3.21 Prompting of Getting Passports Ready for Check(提示乘客持护照下机接受检查) 170
- 7.3.22 Reporting a Theft Case to the Security Authorities(偷盗报案) 171

Words and Expressions 171

Practice 172

Unit 8　Emergency Announcements 179

8.1　Fire in the Cabin(客舱失火) 179
- 8.1.1 Decompression(客舱释压) 179
- 8.1.2 Announcement of the Cabin Fire(客舱失火通告) 179
- 8.1.3 Fire Extinguished(灭火后) 180
- 8.1.4 Emergency Landing (Ditching)[陆地(海上)迫降] 180
- 8.1.5 Emergency Announcements(On Behalf of the Captain)[紧急广播(代表机长)] 180

Words and Expressions 181

8.2　Announcements by the Crew Chief(乘务长广播) 181
- 8.2.1 Cabin Tidying and Seatback/Table Fastening(客舱整理、固定好座椅靠背/小桌板) 181
- 8.2.2 Introduction to the Exit(紧急出口介绍) 182
- 8.2.3 Aid Donors Selection(选择援助者) 182
- 8.2.4 Taking Away Sharp Objects(取下尖锐物品) 182
- 8.2.5 Safety Position(防冲击姿势说明) 183
- 8.2.6 Demonstration of the Usage of a Life Vest(救生衣使用演示) 183
- 8.2.7 Safety Instructions Leaflet(安全说明书) 184
- 8.2.8 Security Tips(安全提示) 184
- 8.2.9 Cabin Lights Dimming(调暗客舱灯光) 185
- 8.2.10 Upper Deck Exits Boeing 747(B747 飞机上舱紧急出口) 185
- 8.2.11 Before Emergency Landing(着陆前防冲击警告广播) 185

Words and Expressions 185

Practice 186

Unit 9　Airport Announcements(机场广播) 192

- 9.1 Paging Departure(登机广播) 192
- 9.2 Commencement of Check-in(办理登机手续广播) 192
- 9.3 Check-in Closing(登机手续即将完毕广播) 192
- 9.4 Commencement of Boarding(开始登机广播) 193
- 9.5 Final Boarding Call(登机最后一次广播) 194
- 9.6 Boarding Announcement for Delayed Departure(航班延误后的登机广播) 194
- 9.7 Irregularity Delay Due to Weather Indefinite Time(因天气原因，航班非正常延误广播) 195

- 9.8 Irregularity Delay Due to Weather Definite Departure Time(因天气原因航班延误，起飞时间确定的广播) 195
- 9.9 Refreshments Are Offered Due to Delay(因延误而提供免费餐饮的广播) 196
- 9.10 Delay Due to Maintenance(因飞机维修，航班延误的广播) 196
- 9.11 Delay Due to Technical Reasons(因技术原因，航班延误的广播) 196
- 9.12 Anticipated Diversion or Return(航班预计改航或回航的广播) 197
- 9.13 Cancellations(航班取消广播) 197
- 9.14 Connecting Passenger Information(联程航班广播) 198
- 9.15 Boarding Announcement(通知旅客登机广播) 198
- 9.16 Paging for Standby Passenger(通知候补旅客广播) 198
- 9.17 Paging for Claiming Baggage(通知认领行李广播) 198
- 9.18 Customs Clearance(办理结关手续广播) 199
- 9.19 Customs Clearance and Baggage Claim(办理结关手续并认领行李广播) 199
- 9.20 Bus Service Available(班车服务广播) 199
- Words and Expressions 199
- Practice 201

Bibliography(参考文献) 208

Part I

At an Airport

Unit 1　Introductions to a Flight Schedule

(航班行程时刻表介绍)

1.1　24-hour System & 12-hour Clock Time

Normally the time is shown as "**hours: minutes**".

There are two major ways to show the time: "12-hour clock time + A.M./P.M." or "24-hour clock".

24-hour System: with the 24-hour clock, the time is shown as how many hours and minutes since midnight.

12-hour Clock Time+A.M./P.M.: with A.M./P.M., the day is split into the 12 hours running from midnight to noon (the A.M. hours) and the other 12 hours running from noon to midnight (the P.M. hours).

At an Airport — Part 1

> On an airline schedule, the time for departure and arrival is published using the 24-hour system, while in dialogue form the 12-hour clock time is used.

In Denmark, you are supposed to always "write" using the 24-hour clock, but spoken Danish used the 12-hour clock.

Abbreviation	A.M.	P.M.
Meaning	Ante Meridiem Latin for "before midday"	Post Meridiem Latin for "after midday"
Time	Midnight to noon	Noon to midnight
24-hour clock	0:00 to 11:59	12:00 to 23:59

1. How to convert 12-hour clock to 24-hour clock?

For the first hour of the day (12 midnight to 12:59 A.M.), subtract 12 hours.
Examples: 12 Midnight = 0:00
12:35 A.M. = 0:35

From 1:00 A.M. to 12:59 P.M., no change.
Examples: 11:20 A.M. = 11:20
12:30 P.M. = 12:30

From 1:00 PM to 11:59 PM, add 12 hours.
Examples: 4:45 P.M. = 16:45
11:50 P.M. = 23:50

2. How to convert 24-hour clock to 12-hour clock?

For the first hour of the day (0:00 to 0:59), add 12 hours, make it "A.M.".
Examples: 0:10 = 12:10 A.M.
0:40 = 12:40 A.M.

From 1:00 to 11:59, just make it "A.M.".
Examples: 1:15 = 1:15 A.M.
11:25 = 11:25 A.M.

From 12:00 to 12:59, just make it "P.M.".
Examples: 12:10 = 12:10 P.M.
12:55 = 12:55 P.M.

From 13:00 to 23:59, subtract 12 hours, make it "P.M.".
Examples: 14:55 = 2:55 P.M.
23:30 = 11:30 P.M.

Midnight and Noon

"12 A.M." and "12 P.M." can cause confusion.

3. Comparison Chart.

Here is a side-by-side comparison of the 24-hour clock and A.M./P.M.

Example: on the hour		Example: 10 minutes past	
24-hour Clock	A.M./P.M.	24-hour Clock	A.M./P.M.
0:00	12 Midnight	0:10	12:10 A.M.
1:00	1:00 A.M.	1:10	1:10 A.M.
2:00	2:00 A.M.	2:10	2:10 A.M.
3:00	3:00 A.M.	3:10	3:10 A.M.
4:00	4:00 A.M.	4:10	4:10 A.M.
5:00	5:00 A.M.	5:10	5:10 A.M.
6:00	6:00 A.M.	6:10	6:10 A.M.
7:00	7:00 A.M.	7:10	7:10 A.M.
8:00	8:00 A.M.	8:10	8:10 A.M.
9:00	9:00 A.M.	9:10	9:10 A.M.
10:00	10:00 A.M.	10:10	10:10 A.M.
11:00	11:00 A.M.	11:10	11:10 A.M.
12:00	12 Noon	12:10	12:10 P.M.
13:00	1:00 P.M.	13:10	1:10 P.M.
14:00	2:00 P.M.	14:10	2:10 P.M.
15:00	3:00 P.M.	15:10	3:10 P.M.
16:00	4:00 P.M.	16:10	4:10 P.M.
17:00	5:00 P.M.	17:10	5:10 P.M.
18:00	6:00 P.M.	18:10	6:10 P.M.
19:00	7:00 P.M.	19:10	7:10 P.M.
20:00	8:00 P.M.	20:10	8:10 P.M.
21:00	9:00 P.M.	21:10	9:10 P.M.
22:00	10:00 P.M.	22:10	10:10 P.M.
23:00	11:00 P.M.	23:10	11:10 P.M.

4. When someone says it is midnight, what time are they referring to?

The term midnight can be a problem for different people around the world—when midnight is used in a sentence, does this mean it's the beginning or end of the day?

Imagine when you are told that your friends are leaving to go on vacation at "midnight" on the 12th of March, what day should you arrive to say goodbye? Do you get there on the 11th (assuming they leave at the very start of the 12th), or the 12th (assuming they leave at the end of the 12th)?

It is better to express like this.

(1) 11:59 P.M. or 12:01 A.M.

(2) 23:59 or 0:01 (24-hour clock).

This is what the railroads, airlines and military actually do.

5. Read the following form carefully and pay attention to the way of converting orally the following 24-hour clock time into 12-hour clock time.

12-hour Clock Time	Spoken Equivalent	24-hour System	Spoken Equivalent
8:00 a.m.	Eight a.m.	08:00	Zero eight hundred
8:40 a.m.	Eight forty a.m.	08:40	Zero eight forty
10:30 a.m.	Ten thirty a.m.	10:30	Ten thirty
12:00 noon	Twelve noon	12:00	Twelve hundred
2:00 p.m.	Two p.m.	14:00	Fourteen hundred
11:45 p.m.	Eleven forty-five p.m.	23:45	Twenty-three forty-five
12:00 midnight	Twelve midnight	24:00	Twenty-four hundred
0:15 a.m.	Zero fifteen a.m.	00:15	Zero Zero fifteen

1.2 Airport/City Codes(机场代码与城市代码)

An **airport/city code** is a short code used to identify a specific airport or city in English, and three letters are often used to indicate various city/airport names. These letters are known as city/airport codes. IATA airport code (International Air Transport Association Airport Code), a four-letter code, is most commonly known to the public because of its use in reservation, ticketing, and baggage-handling systems.

SHA stands for Shanghai Hongqiao.

HRB stands for Harbin.

1.3 Airline Designator Codes(航空公司代码)

IATA airline designators, sometimes called IATA reservation codes, are two-character codes assigned by the International Air Transport Association (IATA) to the world's airlines.

CA refers to Air China.

CZ refers to China Southern Airlines.

Airline Codes in China(中国航空公司代码)

Logo (标志)	Code (代码)	English Name (英文名)	Chinese Name (中文名)	Explanation(说明)
	CA	Air China	中国国际航空股份有限公司	中国国际航空股份有限公司(简称"国航"),其前身是成立于1988年的中国国际航空公司。根据国务院批准通过的《民航体制改革方案》,2002年10月,中国国际航空公司联合中国航空总公司和中国西南航空公司,成立了中国航空集团公司,并以联合三方的航空运输资源为基础,组建新的中国国际航空公司。2004年9月30日,经国务院国有资产监督管理委员会批准,作为中国航空集团控股的航空运输主业公司,国航股份在北京正式成立。2004年12月15日,中国国际航空股份有限公司在香港(股票代码 0753)和伦敦(交易代码 AIRC)成功上市
	MU	China Eastern Airlines	中国东方航空股份有限公司	中国东方航空股份有限公司(简称"东航")总部位于上海,是我国三大国有骨干航空运输集团之一。2002年,以原东航为主体,在兼并原中国西北航空公司、联合原云南航空公司的基础上,组建成了中国东方航空股份有限公司
	CZ	China Southern Airlines	中国南方航空股份有限公司	中国南方航空股份有限公司是中国南方航空集团公司下属的航空运输主业公司,总部设在广州,以蓝色垂直尾翼镶红色木棉花为公司标志。中国南方航空股份有限公司是国内运输飞机最多、航线网络最密集、年客运量最大的航空公司
	HU	Hainan Airlines	海南航空股份有限公司	海南航空股份有限公司是中国民航第一家A股和B股同时上市的航空公司。该公司于1993年1月由海南省航空公司经规范化股份制改造后建立,1993年5月2日正式开航运营,注册资本7.3亿人民币
	SC	Shandong Airlines	山东航空股份有限公司	被誉为"齐鲁之翼"的山东航空股份有限公司(简称"山航")是由中国国际航空股份有限公司、山东省经济开发投资公司等12家股东组控的从事航空运输相关产业经营的企业集团公司。1994年3月12日经国家民航总局和山东省委、省政府批准,成立"山航",总部设在济南
	FM	Shanghai Airlines	上海航空股份有限公司	上海航空公司成立于1985年,是中国国内第一家多元投资、商业化运营的航空公司。上海航空公司自成立21年来,始终坚持"安全第一,顾客至上,优质服务,追求卓越"的经营宗旨,以"把上海航空公司办成国内最好、顾客首选、具有国际水平的航空公司"为战略目标

At an Airport Part I

Continued(续表)

Logo(标志)	Code(代码)	English Name(英文名)	Chinese Name(中文名)	Explanation(说明)
	ZH	Shenzhen Airlines	深圳航空有限责任公司	深圳航空有限责任公司成立于1992年11月, 1993年9月17日正式开航, 是主要经营航空客、货、邮运输业务的股份制航空运输企业。自开航以来, 深航连续保持了13年营利和14年安全飞行, 以安全飞行、优质服务、良好的经济效益和高效的管理模式赢得了社会的广泛赞誉
	3U	Sichuan Airlines	四川航空股份有限公司	四川航空股份有限公司的前身是四川航空公司, 该公司成立于1986年9月19日, 1988年7月14日正式开航营运。四川航空股份有限公司成立于2002年8月29日, 是以四川航空公司为主, 联合中国南方航空股份有限公司、上海航空股份有限公司、山东航空股份有限公司、成都银杏餐饮有限公司共同发起设立的跨地区、跨行业、跨所有制、投资主体多元化的股份制航空公司
	MF	Xiamen Airlines	厦门航空有限公司	厦门航空有限公司是1984年7月25日成立的全国第一家按企业化运行的航空公司, 自主经营的法人实体, 实行董事会领导下的总经理负责制。现股东为: 中国南方航空股份有限公司(占60%股权)和厦门建发集团有限公司(占40%股权)
	BK	Okay Airways	奥凯航空有限公司	奥凯航空有限公司是中国大陆第一批获得批准成立的民营资本控股的航空公司, 总部位于北京, 主要基地为天津滨海国际机场
	9C	Spring Airlines	春秋航空股份有限公司	春秋航空股份有限公司是首个中国民营资本独资经营的低成本航空公司专线。2011年春秋航空净利润逾4.7亿元, 成为当前国内最成功的低成本航空公司, 总部在上海, 在上海虹桥机场、上海浦东机场、石家庄正定机场、沈阳桃仙机场设有基地。春秋航空股份有限公司经中国民用航空总局批准成立于2004年5月26日, 由春秋旅行社创办, 注册资本8,000万元人民币, 创立之初, 只有3架租赁的空客A320飞机, 经营国内航空客货运输业务和旅游客运包机运输业务。2005年7月18日开通首航。春秋航空平均上座率达到95.4%, 成为国内民航客座率最高的航空公司
	KN	China United Airlines	中国联合航空有限公司	中国联合航空有限公司, 是一家以北京南苑机场(现变更为北京大兴国际机场)为主运营基地的民用商业航空公司, 下设中国联合航空有限公司河北分公司(河北石家庄)、北京南苑联合机场管理服务有限公司(北京南苑)、佛山沙堤机场管理有限公司(广东佛山)。2019年9月26日起, 中国联合航空有限公司整体搬迁至北京大兴国际机场运行

Continued(续表)

Logo(标志)	Code(代码)	English Name(英文名)	Chinese Name(中文名)	Explanation(说明)
	G5	China Express Airlines	华夏航空有限公司	华夏航空有限公司（简称"华夏航空"），是经中国民用航空总局批准成立的一家总部设在贵州省贵阳市的中国国内专门从事支线航空客货运输业务的中外合资航空公司，也是国内首家中外合资的支线航空公司。截至2018年3月共有37架飞机
	8L	Lucky Air	云南祥鹏航空有限责任公司	云南祥鹏航空有限责任公司成立于2004年6月，是经中国民用航空总局批准的，经营云南省内航空客货运输业务及其他国内航空运输业务的公共航空运输企业；系海航集团旗下的控股公司，由海南航空集团有限公司(占67.95%股份)、山西航空公司(占31.38%股份)、云南石林航空旅游公司(占0.67%股份)等三家共同投资组建。2006年2月26日，祥鹏航空开航运营
	HO	Juneyao Airlines	上海吉祥航空有限公司	上海吉祥航空股份有限公司(简称"吉祥航空")，系"中国民企百强"企业——上海均瑶(集团)有限公司控股子公司。吉祥航空以上海为主运营基地和维修基地，以上海虹桥国际机场和浦东国际机场为飞行基地，经营范围包括国内航空客货邮运输、商务旅游包机业务，内地至香港、澳门特别行政区和周边国家的航空客货运输业务
	JD	Beijing Capital Airlines	北京首都航空有限公司	北京首都航空有限公司(简称"首都航空")，是经中国民用航空局及北京市工商行政管理局批准成立的，由海航集团与首旅集团共同出资组建，是海南航空集团旗下的航空公司，于2010年5月2日正式挂牌开航。其前身为成立于1998年的金鹿航空有限公司，基地机场为北京首都国际机场
	GS	Tianjin Airlines	天津航空有限责任公司	天津航空是总部位于天津的一家民用支线航空公司，天津航空公司由海南航空集团有限公司、天津保税区投资有限公司，以及海南航空股份有限公司共同出资组建，于2009年6月8日成立，基地设在天津滨海国际机场。2010年6月1日天津航空获批扩大经营范围，开始经营国内干线航空及国际航空市场
	PN	West Airlines	西部航空有限责任公司	西部航空有限责任公司是经中国民航局批准成立的中国西部地区第二家民营航空公司，注册资本2.4亿元，成立于2006年，是海南航空集团旗下的航空公司。2007年6月14日西部航空公司开航运营，主运营基地位于重庆江北国际机场，经营范围包括国内航空客货运输、航空公司间代理、航空器维修、航空器材进出口、航空配餐服务等

1.4　Aircraft Types(机型)

An aircraft is a vessel designed to move through the air. An airplane is a popular example of this type of vessel, but there are many others. Helicopters, airships, and hot air balloons are also examples of different types of aircraft.

An airplane may be one of the most recognizable types of aircraft. These vessels have fixed wings and propellers. Their body styles can greatly vary as there are many types and sizes of airplanes used for numerous reasons. These include seaplanes and jets.

Most airplanes require a runway for take-off and landing. Seaplanes are an exception. These flying vessels can take off and land on water. One type, known as a floatplane, has floating structures extending from the bottom of the plane's body to prevent it from touching the water. Another type, known as a flying boat, tends to have floating devices under the wings because part of the body rests in the water.

People often mistakenly believe that airplanes and jets are separate types of aircraft. A jet is an airplane but is set apart by the fact that it has jet engines. These engines require different fuels than the engines of many other types of airplanes. Jets tend to be preferable aircraft when flying at high speed and high altitudes over long distances.

Here are examples：

Aircraft Types (机型)	Name(名称)	Aircraft Types (机型)	Name(名称)
M90/M82/M11/D10/M1F	McDonnell Douglas(麦克唐奈·道格拉斯)MD-90/MD-82/MD-11/DC10/MD-11 Frighter	777	Boeing(波音)777
AN4	Antonov(安)24	747	Boeing(波音)747
AB6、ABF	Airbus(空中客车)A300-600R	744	Boeing(波音)747-400P
AB3、AB4	Airbus(空中客车)A300、A300-400	74L	Boeing(波音)747 SP
310、312、313	Airbus(空中客车)A310、A310-200、A310-300	74M	Boeing(波音)747-200
320、321、330、340	Airbus(空中客车)A320、A321、A330、A340	74D	Boeing(波音)747-300
F70、100	Fokker(荷兰福克)70、100	74E	Boeing(波音)747-400
TU5、TU3	Tupolev(图)TU-154、134	74F	Boeing(波音)747F
SH6	Shorts(肖特)360	707、70F、757、752	Boeing(波音)707、707F、757、757-200
DH8、DH6	Dash(冲)8、Dash(冲)6	767、763、762	Boeing(波音)767、767-300、767-200
ILW、IL7	Ilyushin(伊尔)IL-86、IL-76	73F、73M、73S	Boeing(波音)737F、737、737-200
IL6、IL4	Ilyushin(伊尔)IL-62、IL-14	733、734、735	Boeing(波音)737-300、737-400、737-500
146、143、141	Br. Aerospace(英国宇航公司)146、143、141	727	Boeing(波音)727
YK2	Yak-42(雅克-42)	SF3	Saab(萨伯)340
YN7	Yunshuji-7(运-7)	130	大力神 C130
MET	METRO-23(美多-23)		

1.5　Business Class(公务舱)

In the airline industry, business class was originally intended as an intermediate level of service between economy class and first class, but many airlines now offer it as the highest level of service, having eliminated first class seating. Business class is distinguished from other travel classes by the quality of seating, food, drinks, ground service and other amenities. Full business class is usually denoted "J" or "C" with schedule flexibility, but can be many other letters depending on circumstances.

Symbol(符号)	Explanation(说明)
C	Business Class(公务舱)
F	First Class(头等舱)
Y	Economy Class(普通舱)
K	Budget Class(经济舱)

Words and Expressions

airport [ˈeəpɔːt] *n.* 机场；航空站

flight [flaɪt] *n.* (物体的)飞行；航班；飞翔；客机

schedule [ˈʃedjuːl] *n.* 时刻表；进度表；清单，明细表

airline [ˈeəlaɪn] *n.* 航线；航空公司

timetable [ˈtaɪmˌteɪbl] *n.* 交通工具的运行时间表；日程表；课程表

aircraft [ˈeəkrɑːft] *n.* 飞机，航空器

board [bɔːd] *n.* 板；董事会；甲板

vt. 上(船、车或飞机)

vi. (火车、轮船、飞机等)接受乘客

a.m. [ˌeɪˈem] *abbr.* 上午，午前

p.m. [ˌpiːˈem] *abbr.* 下午，午后

departure [dɪˈpɑːtʃə(r)] *n.* 离开，离去；起程；背离

midnight [ˈmɪdnaɪt] *n.* 子夜，午夜

convert [kənˈvɜːt] *vt.* (使)转变；使皈依；兑换，换算

subtract [səbˈtrækt] *vt.* 减去；扣除

assume [əˈsjuːm] *vi.&vt.* 假定，认为；承担；装出；呈现

equivalent [ɪˈkwɪvələnt] *n.* 对等物

code [kəʊd] *n.* [计算机]编码；代号，密码

aviation [ˌeɪviˈeɪʃn] *n.* 航空；飞行术，航空学；飞机制造业；[集合词]飞机

IATA *abbr.* International Air Transport Association 国际航空运输协会

baggage [ˈbæɡɪdʒ] *n.* 行李

designator [ˌdezɪɡˈneɪtə] *n.* 标识；代码

vessel [ˈvesl] *n.* 容器；船，飞船

helicopter [ˈhelɪkɒptə(r)] *n.* 直升飞机

propeller [prəˈpelə(r)] *n.* 螺旋桨，推进器；

floatplane [ˈfləʊtpleɪn] *n.* 飞行艇，水上飞机

jet [dʒet] *n.* 喷嘴，喷雾；喷气式飞机

altitude [ˈæltɪtjuːd] *n.* 高度，海拔高度；高位

preferable [ˈprefrəbl] *adj.* 更好的，更可取的；略胜一筹的

Boeing [ˈbəʊɪŋ] *n.* 波音公司；波音；波音飞机

intermediate [ˌɪntəˈmiːdiət] *adj.* 中间的，中级的

eliminate [ɪˈlɪmɪneɪt] *vt.* 排除，消除；淘汰；除掉

seating [ˈsiːtɪŋ] *n.* 座位；座位数

distinguish [dɪˈstɪŋɡwɪʃ] *vi&vt.* 区分，辨别，分清；辨别是非

flexibility [ˌfleksəˈbɪləti] *n.* 柔韧性，机动性，灵活性；伸缩性

circumstance [ˈsɜːkəmstəns] *n.* 环境，境遇；情况，情形

budget [ˈbʌdʒɪt] *n.* 预算；预算案；预算拨款
adj. 价格低廉的；花钱少的；收费合理的；便宜的

Practice

Ⅰ. Look and Say

Tell the names of the Airlines according to the given logos, both in English and in Chinese, and then identify the airline code of each logo.

At an Airport Part I

Ⅱ. Word Matching

Match the technical terms in Column A with their definitions in Column B.

Column A

- aviation
- timetable
- airport
- board
- jet
- baggage
- flight
- departure
- code
- helicopter

Column B

(1) a schedule listing the times at which certain events, such as the time when the arrivals and departures at a transportation station, are expected to take place(一张列出某些事情的预计时间表，比如交通站中交通工具到达和离开的时间)

(2) the act of leaving(离开的行为)

(3) the trunks, bags, parcels, and suitcases in which one carries one's belongings while traveling; luggage(某人旅行时携带物品的大皮箱、手提包、小包裹和衣箱等)

(4) an aircraft that derives its lift from blades that rotate about an approximately vertical central axis(螺旋桨叶围绕一根近似垂直的中心轴旋转而使其升高的飞机)

(5) the operation of aircraft to provide transportation(操纵飞机)

(6) to enter or go aboard a vehicle or ship(上车或上船)

(7) a system of symbols and rules used to represent instructions to a compute(用于表示计算机指令的符号和规则系统)

(8) a jet-propelled vehicle, especially a jet-propelled aircraft(喷气式机动装置，尤指喷气式飞机)

(9) a tract of leveled land where aircraft can take off and land, usually equipped with hard-surfaced landing strips, a control tower, hangars, aircraft maintenance and refueling facilities, and accommodations for passengers and cargo(可供飞机起飞和降落的场地，通常配有坚硬的飞机跑道、控制塔、飞机库、飞机维护和加油设备以及乘客候机设施和货物贮存地)

(10) a scheduled airline run or trip(按时的航线或旅行)

III. Dialogue Completion

In the following dialogues, some sentences have been removed. Choose the most suitable one from the list to fit into each of the numbered blank, and then work in pairs and act as the customer and reservation clerk according to the dialogue.

Dialogue 1   Reservations

> A. How would you like to pay, Ms. Jones?
> B. The flight number is NWA 476.
> C. Yes. There's one flight at 16:45 and the other one at 18:00.
> D. The flight leaves at 16:45, and your arrival in Sydney will be at 9:25 a.m. local time.
> E. The 16:45, please.
> F. Economy, please.

Reservation clerk: Northwind Airways, good morning. May I help you?

Mary Jones: Yes. Do you have any flights to Sydney next Tuesday afternoon?

Reservation clerk: One moment, please. _____(1)_____

Mary Jones: That's fine. Could you tell me how much a return flight costs? I'll be staying three weeks.

Reservation clerk: Economy, business class or first class ticket?

Mary Jones: _____(2)_____

Reservation clerk: That would be €346.

Mary Jones: OK. Could I make a reservation?

Reservation clerk: Certainly. Which flight would you like?

Mary Jones: _____(3)_____

Reservation clerk: Could I have your name, please?

Mary Jones: My name is Mary Jones, that's M—A—R—Y, J—O—N—E—S.

Reservation clerk: _____(4)_____

Mary Jones: Can I pay at the check-in desk when I pick up my ticket?

Reservation clerk: Yes, but you will have to confirm this reservation at least two hours before departure time.

Mary Jones: I see.

Reservation clerk: Now you have been booked, Ms. Jones. _____(5)_____

Mary Jones: What's the flight number?

Reservation clerk: _____(6)_____

Mary Jones: Thank you.

Dialogue 2　The Flight Schedule

> A. How long does the flight take?
>
> B. The Shanghai-Sydney one-way fare is CNY13310.
>
> C. I'd like some information about your service to Sydney.
>
> D. Oh, no. I haven't decided my date yet.
>
> E. Flight MU561 leaves on Tuesday, Friday, Saturday and Sunday at 9:35 p.m. and arrives at 9:30 a.m.

A: Good morning, sir. May I help you?

B: Hello. _____(1)_____ Schedules, fares and so on.

A: Yes, sir. We have flights from Shanghai to Sydney every day except Monday. _____(2)_____ the next day while Flight CA175 leaves on Wednesday, Thursday and Saturday at 8:00 p.m. and arrives at 9:50 a.m. the next day.

B: _____(3)_____

A: The flying time is about nine hours.

B: What's the economy class fare?

A: _____(4)_____ Would you like to buy a ticket now?

B: _____(5)_____ I'll buy a ticket later. Anyhow, thank you very much.

Ⅳ. Translation and Practice

Translate the following conversations into English, and then practice with your partner.

Dialogue 1

甲：先生，您有事吗？

乙：我想知道 CA981 航班今天什么时候起飞。

甲：我来查一下。该航班今天 21 点起飞。

乙：谢谢。

Dialogue 2

甲：您好，先生。您在看什么呢？

乙：请看那个显示屏。CJ6104 航班的乘客就要登机了。

甲：对。那是另一个飞往沈阳的航班。

乙：这个航班什么时候起飞？

Ⅴ. Situational Practice

Drill according to the information and situation given below.

1. Here is a sample airline timetable and their related instructions.

Days	Dep.	Arr.	Flight	A/C	Stops	Class	R
●1 Beijing To							
●2 Shanghai							
1234567	0845	1025	CA1501	747	1	Y	-
●3	●4	●5	●6 ●7	●8	●9	●10	●11

● 1：Departure city(出发城市)

● 2：Arrival city(到达城市)

● 3：Days 1234567(表示日期，星期一、二、三、四、五、六、日)

● 4：Dep.(Departure time 离站时间，即表中的 0845)

● 5：Arr.(Arrival time 到达时间，即表中的 1025)

● 6：Airline codes(航空公司代号，即表中的 CA)

● 7：Flight(Flight Number 航班号码，即表中的 CA1501)

● 8：A/C(Aircraft 飞机，即表中的 747 型飞机)

● 9：Stops(Number of stopovers 中途停靠站数，即表中的 1)

● 10：Class(Class of service 等级，即表中的 Y)

● 11：R(Remarks 备注，即表中的-)

2. Symbols and abbreviations related instructions.

Symbol(符号)	Explanation(说明)
BW	Biweekly(隔周飞行)
*	Next day(次日)
* *	After two days(第三日)
CG	Cargo(货班)
16/11→31/12	Effective from Nov. 16 to Dec. 31 (11月16日至12月31日飞行)
16/11→	Effective from Nov. 16 (11月16日起飞行)
→31/12	Effective up to Dec. 31 inclusive (飞行至12月31日止)
(3)1/7→	Wed. flight starts from July 1 (周三航班7月1日起飞行)
→1/11←	only effective on Nov. 1 (仅11月1日飞行)
(1)←17/5	Effective on Monday before May 17 (5月17日前周一飞行)
←6—8→	Grounding from June to August. (6月至8月停飞)

Drill (1): A certain passenger comes to your counter to inquire about flight service, and you are expected to tell him or her the time of flights according to the following timetable.

Example: Flight TK21 leaves at 00:10 a.m. and arrives at 08:10 a.m.

Flight No.	Airlines	A/C	Departure	Dep.	Arr.	Frequency
TK21	Turkish Airlines	BOEING 777-300	Istanbul	00:10	08:10	1 2 3 4 5 6 7
CA907	Air China	AIRBUS A330-200	Madrid	00:15	13:35	- - 3 - - 6 -
CA907	Air China	AIRBUS A330-200	Gru	00:15	01:55	- - - 4 - - 7
CA907	Air China	AIRBUS A330-200	Madrid	00:15	13:35	- - - 4 - - 7
J56217	Donghai Airlines	73F	Wuxi	00:20	02:20	1 2 3 4 5 6 -
J56223	Donghai Airlines	73F	Hangzhou	00:25	02:30	1 2 3 4 5 - -
J56215	Donghai Airlines	73F	Shenzhen	00:25	03:35	1 - - - - - 7
J56223	Donghai Airlines	73F	Wuhan	00:25	04:20	1 2 3 4 5 - -
MS956	Egyptair	AIRBUS A330-200	Cairo	00:30	11:30	- 2 - 4 - 6 -
O36865	Sf Airlines	75F	Hangzhou	00:40	02:50	1 2 3 4 5 6 7

At an Airport   Part I

Drill (2): Some passengers come to your counter to inquire about flight service. Work with your partner and create short dialogues based on the following schedule.

BEIJING PEK(北京)

Days	Dep.	Arr.	Flight	A/C	Stops	Class	R
1 - - 4 - - -	08:40	10:50	MU7115	737	-	Y	-
- - - - - 6 -	10:00	12:10	MU5151	FK1	-	Y	-
- 2 - - 5 - 7	10:05	12:15	X2309	737	-	Y	-
- 2 - - 5 - 7	11:00	13:10	CA1548	737	-	Y	-

HARBIN HRB(哈尔滨)

Days	Dep.	Arr.	Flight	A/C	Stops	Class	R
- 2 - - - - -	11:20	15:15	MU7617	737	1	Y	-
- - - 4 - - 7	17:15	21:50	CJ6254	M82	1	FY	-
- - - - 5 - -	17:30	20:05	CJ6286	M82	-	FY	-
- 2 - - - 6 -	18:10	21:15	CJ6236	M82	-	FY	-

NANJING NKG(南京)

Days	Dep.	Arr.	Flight	A/C	Stops	Class	R
- - - - 5 - -	11:50	13:05	MU7705	737	-	Y	-
- 2 - - 5 - -	12:20	14:05	F65921	DH8	-	Y	-
- - - - - - 7	12:30	14:10	MU7510	YK2	-	Y	-
1 - - 4 - - -	15:40	16:50	MU7705	737	-	Y	-

VI. Group Work

Suppose you are a reservation clerk or a customer. Create your dialogue according to the information given below, and act out in the group.

Confirmation of flight reservation.

Reservation clerk: Northwind Airlines. Can I help you?

Customer: _____

Reservation clerk: May I have your name and flight number, please?

Customer: _____

Reservation clerk: When are you leaving?

Customer: _____

Reservation clerk: And your destination?

Customer: _____

Reservation clerk: Hold the line, please. _____ All right. Your seat is confirmed, Mr. Adams. You'll be arriving in Buenos Aires at 4:00 p.m. local time.

Customer: _____

Reservation clerk: Yes, but please check in at least one hour before departure time.

VII. Group Discussions

Form groups of three or four to discuss the following questions. Representatives will be asked to put forward their answers in the front.

(1) What is the difference between a 24-hour system and a 12-hour clock time? Which time system is more commonly used at an airport?

(2) What is the capital city of your province? What is the name of the airport in your home town? Do you know the city and airport codes?

(3) Which airlines have you heard of? Do you know the designator codes of any airline?

(4) Do you know any aircraft types? What are they?

(5) Do you know the different classes on board at an aircraft? What are they?

Ⅷ. Further Study

1. "飞机"一词的演变

英语中"飞机"一词的命名，与飞机构造中的一个非常重要的组成部分——维持飞机在空中飞行的机翼有关。其演变过程颇为复杂。

Plane 一词起源于 17 世纪的拉丁语 planu，意为"平坦的表面"。

Aeroplane 一词出现在 1866 年，由前缀 aero-(意为"空气，航空")和意指保持飞行器在高空飞行的结构的单词 plane 组成。由于当时飞机还没有被发明出来，所以在这些带有想象的文章中，Aeroplane 还没有飞机的意思。并且在这些文章中机翼被作者想象成是平坦的，因此作者在表述时选用了单词 plane；而实际情况是，真正的机翼，表面是弯曲的(这是人们从后来的飞行试验中得出的结果)。直到 1873 年，才首次出现了 aeroplane 一词具有"飞行器"之义的记载。

1903 年，随着人类第一架依靠自身动力进行载人飞行的飞机——"飞行者 1 号"的诞生，人们对飞机的普遍认识发生了巨大飞跃。

于是，1907 年具有现代飞机意思的单词 airplane，首次出现在文献记录中，它使用 air- 代替了 aero-。

1908 年 4 月带有"有翼的飞行器"之意的 plane，首次出现在文献记录中。但从这些文章的上下文内容来看，此时的 plane 仅表示的是 aeroplane 的缩写形式，即它也没有飞机的意思。

1908 年 6 月，具有"飞机"之意的 plane 一词，首次出现在《伦敦时报》中一段提及赖特先生的引文中。

此后，美国人在表述他们的飞行时，使用的单词是 airplane；而英国人在表述他们的飞行时，使用的单词仍然是 aeroplane，但他们乘坐的都是同一种事物——plane。当然，甚至有时一个美国人和一个英国人，会乘坐同一架 plane。这种情况，最终促使 plane 逐渐具有了"飞机"的意思。

2. 飞机场：airport，aerodrome(或 airdrome)，airfield 辨析

(1) airport 不仅设有货运或客运设施、燃料供给设施，而且还设有海关机构。

The plane was late and the detectives were waiting at the airport all morning. 那班飞机晚点了，几个侦探整个上午一直守在机场。

(2) aerodrome 是英式英语词汇，airdrome 是美式英语词汇，与 airport 同义，并逐渐被 airport 取代。

I live near an airport and passing planes can be heard night and day. 我住在一个飞机场附

近,白天黑夜都能听到飞机飞过的声音。

(3) airfield 是飞机场供飞机起飞或降落的区域。

When the plane arrived, some of the detectives were waiting inside the main building while others were waiting on the airfield. 飞机到达时,一些侦探等候在主楼里,而另一些则等候在飞机降落的地方。

Soon afterwards, the balloon began to descend and it landed near an airfield. 随后,那只热气球开始下降,它在附近的一个机场着陆。

Airport

Airfield

3. 12 小时制和 24 小时制

12 小时制的时间规则是把一日 24 小时分为两个时段，分别为上午(a.m.，拉丁文 ante meridiem 表示中午之前)和下午(p.m.，拉丁文 post meridiem 表示中午之后)；每个时段均由 12 个小时构成，以数字 12、1、2、3、4、5、6、7、8、9、10、11 依次序表示；上午时段由午夜至中午，而下午时段由中午至午夜。

尽管在现代世界中 12 小时制已经被 24 小时制广泛代替，尤其是在书写通信中。但是，12 小时制使用的 a.m./p.m.形式仍然是当前澳大利亚和美国在书写、交谈时使用的主要形式。

另外，在加拿大(尤其是魁北克)、英联邦、阿尔巴尼亚、希腊和其他的英语地区，以及南美洲的西班牙语地区，12 小时制也是常常和 24 小时制同时使用。

同 24 小时制相比，12 小时制常常被反对者提到的缺点如下。

(1) 容易混淆正午和深夜的时间。
(2) 容易混淆在凌晨时间的正确日期。
(3) 在排版时要输入 a.m.或 p.m.，占用的空间更多。

24 小时制	12 小时制
00:00	上午 12:00
01:00	上午 1:00
02:00	上午 2:00
03:00	上午 3:00
04:00	上午 4:00
05:00	上午 5:00
06:00	上午 6:00
07:00	上午 7:00
08:00	上午 8:00
09:00	上午 9:00
10:00	上午 10:00
11:00	上午 11:00
12:00	下午 12:00
13:00	下午 1:00
14:00	下午 2:00
15:00	下午 3:00
16:00	下午 4:00
17:00	下午 5:00
18:00	下午 6:00
19:00	下午 7:00
20:00	下午 8:00
21:00	下午 9:00
22:00	下午 10:00
23:00	下午 11:00
00:00	上午 12:00

24 小时制的时间规则是把一日的时间分为 24 个小时，从数字 0～23(24 是每日完结的午夜)依次序表示。这个时间记录系统是现今全世界最常用的时制。24 小时制在美国和加拿大被称为军事时间，而在英国则被称作大陆时间。此外，24 小时制还是国际标准时间系统(ISO 8601)。

24 小时制的时间书写的格式为"小时:分钟"(如 01:23)，或者为"小时:分钟:秒"(如 01:23:45)。对于当前时间不足 10 的数字，在其前面要补充一个零。这个零在小时部分并不是必不可少的，但使用却非常广泛。在 24 小时之中，一天开始于午夜，即 00:00，每天的最后一分钟开始于 23:59，而结束于 24:00。某一天的 24:00 等同于其下一天的 00:00。另外，数字时钟在显示 24 小时制时是从 00:00 到 23:59，它从不会显示出 24:00。这样，从 23:59:59.999 到 00:00:00.000 就可以精确地确定新一天的开始和结束时间。

24 小时制对于需要全天 24 小时运作的机构尤为重要，如航空公司、铁路和军队。

4．国际航空运输协会

国际航空运输协会(International Air Transport Association，IATA)是一个由世界各国航

空公司所组成的大型国际组织，其前身是 1919 年在海牙成立，并在二战时解体的国际航空业务协会，总部设在加拿大的蒙特利尔，执行机构设在日内瓦。和监管航空安全和航行规则的国际民航组织相比，IATA 更像是一个由承运人(航空公司)组成的国际协调组织，管理在民航运输中出现的诸如票价、危险品运输等问题。

IATA 在组织形式上是一个航空企业的行业联盟，属非官方性质组织，但是由于世界上的大多数国家的航空公司属国家所有，即使非国有的航空公司也受到所属国政府的强力干预或控制，因此 IATA 实际上是一个半官方组织。它制定运价的活动，也必须在各国政府授权下进行，它的清算所对全世界联运票价的结算是一项有助于世界空运发展的公益事业，因而 IATA 发挥着通过航空运输企业来协调和沟通政府间政策，解决实际运作困难的重要作用。

IATA 的宗旨是"为了世界人民的利益，促进安全、正常和经济的航空运输，扶植航空交通，并研究与此有关的问题；对直接或间接从事国际航空运输工作的各空运企业提供合作的途径；与国际民航组织及其他国际组织协力合作"。

1993 年 8 月，中国国际航空公司、中国东方航空公司和中国南方航空公司加入了 IATA。1994 年 4 月 15 日，IATA 在北京设立了中国代理人事务办事处。1995 年 7 月 21 日，中国国际旅行社总社正式加入 IATA，成为 IATA 在中国大陆的首家代理人会员。国旅总社在取得 IATA 指定代理人资格后，便有权使用国际航协代理人的专用标志，可取得世界各大航空公司的代理权，使用国际航协的统一结算系统，机票也同世界通用的客票相同。1997 年 3 月 3 日，中国西南航空公司正式成为 IATA 的多边联运协议成员 MITA。MITA 的主要职能是为成员航空公司进行旅客、行李、货物的接收、中转、更改航程及其他相关程序提供统一的标准，成员航空公司间可互相销售而不必再签双边联运协议。全球共有 300 家航空公司加入 MITA。中国西南航空公司是继中国国航、东航、南航之后，第四家成为 MITA 成员的航空运输企业。

5. 波音系列飞机

波音系列飞机是美国波音公司拥有的一个非常成功的民用运输机产品系列，主要机型有波音 2707、波音 247、波音 307、波音 377、波音 707、波音 717、波音 727、波音 737、波音 747、波音 757、波音 767、波音 777、波音 787 等。

1958 年，波音公司生产了波音 707 飞机，它采用了涡轮喷气发动机，不但提高了飞机的飞行速度和飞行高度，而且增大了载客量和航程，是第一代喷气民用运输机。在改进喷气发动机技术后，出现了高流量比涡轮风扇发动机。1963 年波音公司将它用作动力装置，生产了波音 727 飞机。该飞机具有耗油率低，发动机噪声小，起飞着陆性能较好等优点。波音 727 属第 2 代喷气民用运输机。早期生产的型号有波音 727-100、727-100C、727-100QC 等，现已停产。目前仍在生产的机型有波音 727-200。这是一种加长型，最多可载乘客 189 人。此外还有改进的波音 727-200 和 727-100C。前者增加了载油量，加大了航程；后者为客货两用型。1967 年，波音公司根据对短程航线需要的估计，生产了波音 737 短程运输机。1968 年，首架波音 747 出厂，1969 年试飞成功并获得通航证。它是一种装 4 台涡轮风扇发动机的宽机身远程客机。其客舱内座椅安排为双过道，最多可载乘客 550 人，属于以宽机身为主要特征的第 3 代喷气民用运输机。1978 年，波音公司相继研制波音 757、波音 767 系列的中等运载能力和中等航程的民用运输机，并于 20 世纪 80 年代生产和投入航线飞行。它们装有两台涡轮风扇发动机，可载乘客 200～300 人。1990 年，波音公司研制出的波音 777 型飞机，是民用航空历史上最大的双发喷气飞机。

2007 年 7 月 8 日，波音公司在西雅图波音总部举行 787 梦想飞机下线仪式。这标志着波音系列飞机又进入了一个新的发展阶段。

Part II

Conversations on Board

Unit 2　　Service on Board(机上服务)

2.1　Greeting and Assisting to the Seat(登机引导)

1. Good afternoon, sir. Welcome aboard. Would you like me to take you to your seat?
2. Good morning, madam. How are you today? Would you like me to show you to your seat?
3. It's a pleasure to see you again. May I show you to your seat?
4. Good afternoon, madam. It's nice to see you again. May I assist you to your seat?

2.2　Jackets or Coats(挂衣服)

1. May I assist you with your jacket, sir?
2. Sir, may I hang your jacket in the closet?
3. Excuse me, sir, would you like me to take your coat?
4. Are there any valuable items in the pockets that you would like to keep with you?
5. I will bring it back to you before landing.

2.3　Hot Towels(热毛巾)

1. Excuse me, sir, would you care for a hot towel? Here you are. Please be careful, it's hot.
2. Sorry to disturb you, sir. May I offer you a hot towel? The towel is quite hot. Please be careful.

2.4　Drinks(迎宾饮料)

1. Excuse me, sir, welcome aboard. Would you care for a drink? (Would you like something to drink?) Today we have orange juice, mineral water and champagne.
2. (旅客选好饮料后) A glass of champagne, certainly.
3. It's nice to see you on board today, sir. May I offer you a drink? Would you like a glass of chilled champagne, orange juice, mineral water, or would you prefer to try one of our (specially made) cocktails?
4. I hope you enjoy your drink.

Conversations on Board Part II

2.5 Offering Pajamas, Slippers and Amenity Kits (提供休闲服、拖鞋、盥洗包)

1. Sir, we have prepared pajamas for you in order to make you feel more comfortable on this flight.

2. Sir, here is our new casual wear for you. What size do you prefer?

3. Sir, I'm sorry, that size is not available. May I offer you a ...(size) instead?

4. Sir, we have prepared slippers for you to make you feel more comfortable during the flight. May I open it for you now?

5. Well then, I'll put the slippers into the seat pocket in front of you for your convenience.

6. Madam, would you care for a L'OCCITANE amenity kit?

7. Madam, may I present you with a complimentary amenity kit by L'OCCITANE?

2.6 Newspapers(送报纸)

1. Excuse me, sir, we have a wide selection. Would you like...?

2. Sir, may I offer you a newspaper or a magazine? We have...

3. Excuse me, sir, would you care for a newspaper? We have *Economics Daily* and *China Daily*. Besides newspapers, we have a selection of magazines as well.

2.7 Menu Introduction(介绍餐谱)

Sir, my name is Jerry. I'm glad to be at your service. Here is the menu, wine list and tea list. Three main course options are shown on this page. Please take a look at the menu first. I will be back to take your order later.

2.8 Drinks Offer(侍酒饮)

1. Sir, may I offer you a cocktail or perhaps a glass of wine?

2. I'm sorry to disturb you, sir. Would you like a drink? We have a selection of alcoholic and non-alcoholic beverages.

3. Excuse me, sir, may I offer you something to drink? We have a selection of wine, cocktails, and soft drinks.

4. Would you like a cocktail, sir? I'd like to recommend our signature cocktails, the Dream of Jiangnan and the Dancing Phoenix with Auspicious Clouds. We also have champagne and a wide selection of wine.

5. Sir, may I offer you a glass of wine to accompany your fried cod fish?

6. Would you care for a glass of wine with your lunch, sir? We have a selection of white and red wine to compliment your meal.

7. May I offer you a glass of wine to go with your dinner? We have a fine selection of red and white wine.

8. May I offer you another glass of Spirit of Nature?

9. Sir, would you like to continue with your wine or another selection?

10. Excuse me, sir, would you like to taste this wine?

11. Thank you, may I top up for you?

2.9　Clearing Glasses(收杯子)

1. Excuse me, sir, how was your cocktail?

2. Excuse me, sir, did you enjoy your cocktail? I'm glad you enjoyed it.

3. I'm happy to hear you like the wine.

4. It is a popular choice.

5. Would you care for another glass?

6. May I clear your glass?

7. May I clear your table?

8. May I prepare your table for dinner?

9. May I lay the linen for you now?

10. I will come back in a moment to prepare your table for dinner.

11. I will serve your drink as soon as possible.

2.10　If a Passenger Doesn't Like the Wine
　　　 (如果旅客不喜欢这款酒)

1. I'm sorry it's not to your liking. Would you like to select another one?

2. May I show you the wine list again to get another selection?

3. I'm sorry you don't like this wine. Would you like to try a new bottle or a different

selection?

4. I'm sorry you don't like this choice. May I offer you Petit Chablis from the north of Burgundy instead?

2.11 Table Preparation(摆餐桌)

1. Sir, may I prepare your table now? Thank you.
2. Sir, we are about to start the dinner service. May I prepare your table?
3. Sir, may I set your table for the dinner service?
4. Sir, may I dress your table for lunch?
5. May I layout your cutlery now?

2.12 Meals(供餐)

1. Madam, may I serve you the main course now?
2. Sir, did you enjoy your fried cod fish?
3. Thank you. Shall I prepare your table for cheese and dessert?
4. I'm happy/glad to hear that. Would you like to continue with cheese and dessert?
5. We will be serving cheese and fruit soon. Perhaps you'd like that?

2.13 Closure(开餐结束语)

1. Enjoy your meal/lunch/dinner please.
2. I hope you enjoy your lunch, sir.
3. Bon/good appetite.

2.14 Tray Collection(收餐盘)

1. Was the meal to your liking, sir? May I prepare your table for cheese and dessert?
2. Excuse me, Ms. Ana, how was your dinner?

2.15 Collection(整理餐桌)

1. Sir, may I offer you another cup of coffee or tea?
2. Sir, did you enjoy your dessert?

3. Thank you. May I clear your table?

4. Excuse me, sir, how was your orange chocolate mousse cake?

5. I'm glad you enjoyed it. Please excuse me while I clear your table.

2.16　In-flight Refreshments (点心服务)

Snacks are available throughout the flight. Anytime you need them, just let me know.

2.17　Headsets(耳机)

1. Excuse me, sir, here is the entertainment system guide. May I offer you a headset?

2. Hope you'll enjoy our in-flight programs.

2.18　Making the Bed(铺床)

1. Sir, would you like to have a rest now? Let me make the bed for you.

2. Here is the quilt which will make you feel warm and comfortable.

3. Sir, may I help you make your bed now or later?

4. Have a good rest/night.

2.19　Communication after the Rest(醒后沟通)

1. Good morning, sir, how was your rest? Here is the hot towel. Would you like some iced orange juice or mineral water to refresh yourself?

2. Good morning. Did you have a good sleep, sir? May I offer you something to drink?

3. Good morning, madam. Did you have a good rest? We have prepared toothpaste and mouthwash for you in the amenity kit.

2.20　Offering CIQ Forms(提供 CIQ 表格)

1. Excuse me, sir, may I offer you a landing card/an arrival form? Thank you.

2. May I offer you a landing card? Thank you.

Words and Expressions

mineral [ˈmɪnərəl] *n.* 矿物，矿石；矿物质

champagne [ʃæmˈpeɪn] *n.* 香槟酒

pajama [pəˈdʒɑːmə] *n.* 睡衣，宽长裤

available [əˈveɪləbl] *adj.* 可获得的；有空的

slipper [ˈslɪpə(r)] *n.* 拖鞋，室内便鞋

convenience [kənˈviːniəns] *n.* 方便，便利；便利设施；个人的舒适或便利；公共厕所

L'OCCITANE 欧舒丹，是一家专门制造及售卖个人护理产品的国际零售企业，主要生产基地设于法国马诺斯克(Manosque)。

amenity [əˈmiːnəti] *n.* 愉快；礼仪，举止；(环境等的)舒适；便利设施

kit [kɪt] *n.* 成套用品；配套元件

compliment [ˈkɒmplɪmənt] *n.* 夸奖；恭维；敬意；道贺，贺词
               vt. 称赞，赞美

complimentary [ˌkɒmplɪˈmentəri] *adj.* 表示敬意的；赞美的；恭维的；赠送的

option [ˈɒpʃn] *n.* 选择(的自由)；选项；选择权

alcoholic [ˌælkəˈhɒlɪk] *adj.* 酒精的，含酒精的；喝酒引起的

non-alcoholic 不含酒精的

beverage [ˈbevərɪdʒ] *n.* 饮料

cocktail [ˈkɒkteɪl] *n.* 鸡尾酒；餐前开胃菜；混合物

recommend [ˌrekəˈmend] *vt.* 推荐；劝告

signature [ˈsɪgnətʃə] *n.* 签名；署名；识别标志，鲜明特征

auspicious [ɔːˈsɪʃəs] *adj.* 有前途的；有希望的；有利的；吉利的

accompany [əˈkʌmpəni] *vt.* 陪伴，陪同；附加，补充；伴随

clear [klɪə] *vt.* 清理；清除；清扫

top up 给……加满

Burgundy [ˈbɜːgəndɪ] *n.* 勃艮第(法国东南部地方的地名，该地产的红葡萄酒)

dessert [dɪˈzɜːt] *n.* 餐后甜食；甜点

refreshment [rɪˈfreʃmənt] *n.* 提神，精神恢复；点心和饮料，茶点

cutlery [ˈkʌtləri] *n.* (刀、叉等)餐具

closure [ˈkləʊʒə] *n.* 关闭；结束

mousse [muːs] *n.* 奶油冻

in-flight *adj.* 飞行途中提供的

headset ['hedset] *n.* (头戴式)耳机，耳麦

entertainment [ˌentəˈteɪnmənt] *n.* 娱乐，消遣

make the bed 铺床，整理床铺

quilt [kwɪlt] *n.* 被子，棉被

mouthwash [ˈmaʊθwɒʃ] *n.* 漱口水

CIQ *abbr.* Custom, Immigration, Quarantine 海关移民局检疫

Practice

Ⅰ. Look and Say

Tell the names of the items according to the given pictures, both in English and in Chinese.

1

2

3

4

5

6

ENTRY CARD — FOR FOREIGN TRAVELLERS

PLEASE COMPLETE IN ENGLISH, FILL IN ☐ WITH ✓

Family Name		Date of Birth	YEAR / MONTH / DAY
Given Names			Male ☐ / Female ☐
Passport No.		Nationality	
Visa No.		**Your Main Reason for Coming to China (one only)**	
Place of Visa Issuance		Convention / Conference ☐ Business ☐	
Flight No. Ship Name Train No.		Employment ☐ Settle down ☐	
		Visiting friends or relatives ☐	
From		Outing /in leisure ☐ Study ☐	
		Return home ☐ Others ☐	
Intended Address in China			

I declare the information I have given is true, correct and complete. I understand incorrect or untrue answer to any questions may have serious consequences.

SIGNATURE

Date of Entry: YEAR / MONTH / DAY

OFFICIAL USE ONLY

证件种类　签证种类

出入境管理局　公安部监制

II. Word Matching

Match the words in Column A with their definitions in Column B.

Column A

- option
- assist
- available
- beverage
- auspicious
- complimentary
- alcoholic
- convenience
- amenity
- recommend

Column B

(1) to give help or support to, especially as a subordinate or supplement; aid (给……帮助或支持，尤指作为隶属或补充)

(2) present and ready for use; at hand; accessible(可用的；现实可用的；手边的；可获得的)

(3) the quality of being suitable to one's comfort, purposes, or needs(适合某人的舒适、目的或需要的性质)

(4) the quality of being pleasant or attractive; agreeableness(使人愉快或吸引人的性质；使人愉快)

(5) expressing, using, or resembling a compliment(表达、运用或类似赞美方式的)

(6) the act of choosing(选择的行为)

(7) related to or resulting from alcohol(与酒精有关的或由酒精制成的)

(8) any one of various liquids for drinking, usually excluding water(任一种饮用的液体，通常不包括水在内)

(9) to praise or commend (one) to another as being worthy or desirable; endorse(向另外一个人称赞或推荐(某人或物)，认为其有价值或合人心意)

(10) attended by favorable circumstances; propitious(伴随着有利情况的；有利的)

III. Dialogue Completion

In the following dialogues, some sentences have been removed. Choose the most suitable one from the list to fit into each of the numbered blank, and then work in pairs and act as the passenger and the crew according to the dialogue.

Conversations on Board Part II

Dialogue 1

> A. Thank you.
> B. And our menu offers a selection of Asian and Western cuisine.
> C. May I offer you the menu and wine list now?

Crew: Excuse me, sir, I'm sorry to disturb you. _____(1)_____

Passenger: Yes, sure.

Crew: Thank you. Here is our wine list which features a wide selection of fine international wine. _____(2)_____

Passenger: Great, thank you.

Crew: Please take a look at it first and I will come back to take your order later. __(3)__

Dialogue 2

> A. Which one would you prefer?
> B. Would you care to sample the wine, sir?
> C. Sir, may I offer you something to drink? We have wine, cocktails, fresh juices, and soft drinks.
> D. Please enjoy your drink, sir.

Crew: Excuse me, _____(1)_____

Passenger: Yes, I'll have a glass of white wine, please.

Crew: Certainly. For white wine, one selection is from Languedoc, and the other one is from Bordeaux. _____(2)_____

Passenger: The Bordeaux, thanks.

Crew: That would be Chateau Jacquet 2008. (While pouring a little wine in the passenger's glass) _____(3)_____

Passenger: Thank you. (After a sip) It's very nice.

Crew: I'm glad you like it. It's a popular choice. _____(4)_____

Dialogue 3

> A. May I prepare your table for dinner?
> B. Would you care for another glass?
> C. Sir, how was your cocktail?

Crew: Excuse me, _____(1)_____

Passenger: It's very nice.

Crew: Thank you. _____(2)_____

Passenger: No, thank you.

Crew: Certainly. _____(3)_____

Passenger: Yes, please. I am hungry.

Ⅳ. Translation and Practice

1. Translate the following sentences into English.

(1) 根据您选择的主菜，特别向您推荐最新的几款优质法国葡萄酒。这是今年特别聘请法国最知名的 3 位品酒师为头等舱旅客精选的法国 AOC 级的葡萄酒。

_____
_____
_____
_____

(2) 先生，我们今天配备了两款进口的白葡萄酒，都产自法国。一款是产自朗格多克区的自然之春干白，一款是产自波尔多区的雅戈酒庄 2008 干白，您看您选用哪种呢？

_____
_____
_____
_____

(3) 先生，今天我们为您准备了两种霞多丽葡萄酒，它们都产自法国的勃艮第地区。这瓶是产自勃艮第南部马丁酒庄的勃艮第一级佳酿 2008 干白，这瓶是产自勃艮第北部地区的小夏布利干白。

_____

_____

_____

(4) 先生，您选的这款小夏布利干白曾在 2009 年伦敦德康特世界葡萄酒大赛中获得过铜奖。伦敦德康特世界葡萄酒大赛是全世界最重要的葡萄酒大赛之一，尤其偏重白葡萄酒，因此这是一款不可多得的好酒。

_____

_____

_____

2. Now, check your answers, and then practice with your partner to make up short dialogues according to the translated sentences.

(1) May I recommend the wine to go with your main course? We have a variety of AOC level French wine that are selected for our distinguished first class passengers by three wine tasters.

(2) Sir, we have two kinds of French white wine. One is Spirit of Nature produced in the Domaine de Petit Ruby in Languedoc, and the other is Bordeaux Blanc, Chateau Jacquet 2008. Which one would you prefer?

(3) Sir, we have two kinds of wine made of Chardonnay, which are both produced in Burgundy. One is Bourgogne Premiere Cuvee, Domaine Martin 2008 from the south of Burgundy, and the other is Petit Chablis White Wine from the north of Burgundy.

(4) Mr. Petit Chablis won Bronze at Decanter World Wine Awards in London in 2009, which is one of the most important international wine awards, especially for white wine. Therefore, it's a superb wine and really worth tasting.

Ⅴ. Individual Work

Figure out the meaning of words that you don't know in the following CIQ forms and try to complete them.

Conversations on Board Part II

DEPARTMENT OF HOMELAND SECURITY
U.S. Customs and Border Protection
OMB No. 1651-0111

欢迎光临美利坚合众国
I-94 入/出境记录
填写说明

除美国公民、返回美国并在美国有居留权的外国侨民、持有移民签证的外国侨民以及访问美国或经由美国过境的加拿大公民外，所有其他旅客均必须填写此表。

请打字或用圆珠笔全部以大写字母清楚填写。请用英语。不得在本表背面书写。

本表由两部分组成。入境记录（第1-17项）和出境记录（第18-21项）均须填写。

所有项目填写完毕后，请将此表交给 CBP 官员。

第9项 - 若由陆路进入美国，请在此空格内填写 **LAND**。
若乘船进入美国，请在此空格内填写 **SEA**。

关于 5 U.S.C. § 552a(e)(3) 隐私法案的通知：本表格系据美国法典第 8 条，包括 INA (8 U.S.C. 1103, 1187) 以及 8 CFR 235.1, 264 和 1235.1 的要求收集资料，此项收集的目的在于告知允许入境的条件，并对非移民外国人抵达和离开美国进行记录。本表格收集的资料可出于执法的目的提供给政府机构，或协助国土安全部 (DHS) 确定您是否可以入境。所有寻求进入美国的非移民外国人，若非得到豁免，必须提供此类资料，否则可导致被拒绝进入美国并遣解出境。

CBP Form I-94 (05/08)
OMB No. 1651-0111

入境记录

入境号码

369078610 22

1. 姓
2. 名
3. 出生日期（日/月/年）
4. 国籍
5. 性别（男或女）
6. 护照颁发日期（日/月/年）
7. 护照到期日期（日/月/年）
8. 护照号码
9. 航空公司和航班号
10. 居住国
11. 登机国
12. 核发签证城市
13. 核发签证日期（日/月/年）
14. 您在美国逗留期间的地址（街名和门牌号码）
15. 所在美国城市和州名
16. 可以在美国与您联系的电话号码
17. 电子邮件地址

CBP Form I-94 (05/08)

DEPARTMENT OF HOMELAND SECURITY
U.S. Customs and Border Protection
OMB No. 1651-0111

出境记录

入境号码

369078610 22

18. 姓
19. 名
20. 出生日期（日/月/年）
21. 国籍

CBP Form I-94 Chinese (05/08)
请见另一面   STAPLE HERE

DEPARTMENT OF HOMELAND SECURITY
U.S. Customs and Border Protection
OMB No. 1651-0111

Welcome to the United States
I-94 Arrival/Departure Record
Instructions

This form must be completed by all persons except U.S. Citizens, returning resident aliens, aliens with immigrant visas, and Canadian Citizens visiting or in transit.

Type or print legibly with pen in ALL CAPITAL LETTERS. Use English. Do not write on the back of this form.

This form is in two parts. Please complete both the Arrival Record (Items 1 through 17) and the Departure Record (Items 18 through 21).

When all items are completed, present this form to the CBP Officer.

Item 9 - If you are entering the United States by land, enter LAND in this space. If you are entering the United States by ship, enter SEA in this space.

5 U.S.C. § 552a(e)(3) Privacy Act Notice: Information collected on this form is required by Title 8 of the U.S. Code, including the INA (8 U.S.C. 1103, 1187), and 8 CFR 235.1, 264, and 1235.1. The purposes for this collection are to give the terms of admission and document the arrival and departure of nonimmigrant aliens to the U.S. The information solicited on this form may be made available to other government agencies for law enforcement purposes or to assist DHS in determining your admissibility. All nonimmigrant aliens seeking admission to the U.S., unless otherwise exempted, must provide this information. Failure to provide this information may deny you entry to the United States and result in your removal.

CBP Form I-94 (05/08)
OMB No. 1651-0111

Arrival Record

Admission Number

275983374 24

1. Family Name
2. First (Given) Name
3. Birth Date (DD/MM/YY)
4. Country of Citizenship
5. Sex (Male or Female)
6. Passport Issue Date (DD/MM/YY)
7. Passport Expiration Date (DD/MM/YY)
8. Passport Number
9. Airline and Flight Number
10. Country Where You Live
11. Country Where You Boarded
12. City Where Visa Was Issued
13. Date Issued (DD/MM/YY)
14. Address While in the United States (Number and Street)
15. City and State
16. Telephone Number in the U.S. Where You Can Be Reached
17. Email Address

CBP Form I-94 (05/08)

DEPARTMENT OF HOMELAND SECURITY
U.S. Customs and Border Protection
OMB No. 1651-0111

Departure Record

Admission Number

275983374 24

18. Family Name
19. First (Given) Name
20. Birth Date (DD/MM/YY)
21. Country of Citizenship

CBP Form I-94 (05/08)
See Other Side   STAPLE HERE

U.S. Customs and Border Protection

Customs Declaration
19 CFR 122.27, 148.12, 148.13, 148.110, 148.111, 1498; 31 CFR 5316

FORM APPROVED
OMB NO. 1651-0009

Each arriving traveler or responsible family member must provide the following information (only ONE written declaration per family is required):

1. Family **Name** _____
   First *(Given)* _____ Middle ____
2. **Birth date** Day ____ Month ____ Year ____
3. Number of **Family members** traveling with you ____
4. (a) U.S. Street **Address** (hotel name/destination) _____
   (b) City _____ (c) State ____
5. **Passport issued by** (country) _____
6. **Passport number** _____
7. Country of **Residence** _____
8. **Countries visited** on this trip prior to U.S. arrival _____
9. **Airline/Flight No.** or Vessel Name _____
10. The primary purpose of this trip is **business**: Yes ☐ No ☐
11. I am (We are) bringing
    (a) fruits, vegetables, plants, seeds, food, insects: Yes ☐ No ☐
    (b) meats, animals, animal/wildlife products: Yes ☐ No ☐
    (c) disease agents, cell cultures, snails: Yes ☐ No ☐
    (d) soil or have been on a farm/ranch/pasture: Yes ☐ No ☐
12. I have (We have) been in close proximity of (such as touching or handling) **livestock**: Yes ☐ No ☐
13. I am (We are) carrying **currency or monetary instruments** over $10,000 U.S. or foreign equivalent: Yes ☐ No ☐
    (see definition of monetary instruments on reverse)
14. I have (We have) **commercial merchandise**: Yes ☐ No ☐
    (articles for sale, samples used for soliciting orders, or goods that are not considered personal effects)
15. **Residents** — the **total value of all goods,** including commercial merchandise I/we have purchased or acquired abroad, (including gifts for someone else, but not items mailed to the U.S.) and am/are bringing to the U.S. is: $ _____

    Visitors — the **total value of all articles** that will remain in the U.S., including commercial merchandise is: $ _____

Read the instructions on the back of this form. Space is provided to list all the items you must declare.

I HAVE READ THE IMPORTANT INFORMATION ON THE REVERSE SIDE OF THIS FORM AND HAVE MADE A TRUTHFUL DECLARATION.

X _____
(Signature)   Date (day/month/year)

For Official Use Only

CBP Form 6059B (10/07)

Ⅵ. Further Study

霞多丽葡萄酒

霞多丽(Chardonnay)葡萄,是白葡萄中的皇后。它的魅力在于其多变的风格和较强的适应性,在任何气候条件下,它的质量始终如一。从寒凉的法国北部的 Chablis 到炎热的阿根廷的 Mendoza 和南澳大利亚的 Barossa Valley,霞多丽呈现出从带有柑橘类水果到充满热带水果和异国情调的不同风姿。它也是香槟酒和起泡酒调和成分中最重要的一分子。霞多丽具有特制的香气。在寒凉的产地它的酸度较高,因而呈现出柠檬、橙子等柑橘类水果的香气。随着气候的变暖,它会有桃、梨、杏等的香气,以至于在炎热的气候出现菠萝、杧果等热带水果的香气。

霞多丽是世界上风格最多样、种植范围最广泛的酿酒葡萄。它从 20 世纪 90 年代末期在国际上开始流行,不仅仅是因其非常容易种植,长势旺盛,酿成的酒相对温和、圆润的特点,而且因为其酸度不是很高,容易被消费者接受。

它可以用来酿制风格多样的葡萄酒,从酒体丰满浓郁的索诺玛葡萄酒,到酒体轻盈剔透的白中白香槟,都是它的杰作。

Unit 3　　Dealing with Special Situations

(特殊情况处理)

3.1　Case Analysis: The Crew Seems to Be Ignoring Me! (个案分析：乘务员忽略我！)

How would you like to deal with the following situation?

Passenger: I'm really disappointed with your service. I have asked for a drink 3 times and I'm still waiting. The crew seems to be ignoring me!

Communication is a process that you can learn to master and be more effective at carrying out. Understanding the steps of communication is essential to became a better communicator. Once you understand the basic steps, you can make a conscious effort to communicate more effectively. While there are differing opinions as to the steps of communication, a basic five-step communication is the most useful and easiest to understand.

The following are five steps of communication.

(1) Adjust your mindset.

(2) Listen actively.

(3) Repeat their concerns, show empathy and acknowledge anger and apologize.

(4) Present a solution/option and appreciate feedback.

(5) Take action and follow-up assurance.

Step 1: Adjust Your Mindset

Once you're aware that your passenger is unhappy, then your first priority is to put yourself into a customer service mindset.

Conversations on Board

This means that you set aside any feelings you might have or that the situation isn't your fault, or that your passenger has made a mistake, or that he or she is giving you unfair criticism.

All that matters is that you realize that your passenger is upset, and that it's up to you to solve the problem. Adjust your mindset so that you're giving 100 percent of your focus to your passenger, and to the current situation.

Step 2: Listen Actively

The most important step in the whole of this process is listening actively to what your passenger is saying — he wants to be heard, and to air his grievances.

Start the dialogue with a neutral statement, such as **"Let's go over what happened"** or **"Please tell me why you're upset".** This subtly creates a partnership between you and your passenger, and lets him know that you're ready to listen.

Resist the temptation to try to solve the situation right away, or to jump to conclusions about what happened. Instead, let your passenger tell you his or her story. As he's talking, don't plan out what you're going to say until he's done. Otherwise, this isn't active listening!

Also, don't allow anything to interrupt this conversation. Give your passenger all of your attention.

Step 3: Repeat Their Concerns, Show Empathy and Acknowledge Anger and Apologize

Once he's had time to explain why he's upset, repeat his concerns so you're sure that you're addressing the right issue. If necessary, ask questions to make sure that you've identified the problem correctly.

Use calm, objective wording. For example, "As I understand it, you are, quite rightly, upset because we didn't deliver the food that we should have delivered to you on time."

Repeating the problem shows the passenger you were listening, which can help lower his anger and stress levels. More than this, it helps you agree on the problem that needs to be solved.

What's more, you can show your empathy and acknowledgement to the passenger.

—Mr. Leeds, I can appreciate this must be very disappointing for you.

—I can understand why you are feeling so upset.

—I agree that it's not acceptable to be kept waiting for such a long time.

—I understand why you're upset. I would be, too. I'm very sorry that we didn't get the in-flight food to you on time, especially since it's caused these problems.

—Mr. Leeds, I'm terribly sorry to hear that you are disappointed with our service today.

—I apologize that we've kept you waiting, Mr. Leeds.

—Mr. Leeds, I am very sorry that our in-flight service today has not met your expectations.

Step 4: Present a Solution/Option and Appreciate Feedback

Now you need to present the passenger with a solution.

—I will be back with your drink as soon as I can. Would you like some warm nuts to accompany your drink?

—May I know what drink you have requested and I'll be back with it immediately. May I also offer you some cheese and fruit to go with your drink?

Thank passengers for their feedback.

—Thank you for bringing this to my attention. We do appreciate your feedback.

—Thank you for letting me know. We always like to hear comments from our passengers.

Then you could say, "If my solution doesn't work for you, I'd love to hear what will make you happy. If it's in my power I'll get it done, and if it's not possible, we can work on another solution together."

Step 5: Take Action and Follow-up Assurance

Once you've both agreed on a solution, you need to take action immediately. Explain every step that you're going to take to fix the problem to your passenger.

Once the situation has been resolved, follow up with your passenger over the next few hours to make sure that he or she is happy with the resolution. Whenever you can, go above and beyond his or her expectations. For instance, you can send her a hand-written apology, or you can express your follow-up assurance.

—We will do whatever we can to ensure that the rest of your flight is pleasurable.

—I will share your comments with the crew and if there is anything else we can do for you, please do not hesitate to press the call button.

—On behalf of the team, I can assure you that we'll do our best to make this journey pleasant for you. Please let us know if there is anything else we can assist you with during the flight.

Further Tips

It's important to handle difficult customers professionally. Learning how to stay calm and cool under pressure can help you get through challenging situations with grace and professionalism.

If your passenger is especially angry, then talk slowly and calmly, and use a low tone of voice. This will subtly help lower the tension, and ensure that you don't escalate the situation by

Conversations on Board

visibly getting stressed or upset yourself.

3.2 Case Analysis: I Can't Sit by My Colleague! (个案分析：我不能和同事坐在一起！)

How would you like to deal with the following condition?

Passenger: I have been flying Air China for years and now I find I can't sit by my colleague. We were expecting to get a lot of work done on this flight.

1. Acknowledgement

—Mr. Freeman, thank you very much for your support over the years. We appreciate that you've chosen to fly with us.

—It's a pleasure to see you again, Mr. Freeman and I'm sorry for this inconvenience.

2. Empathy

—I can see why you would find it frustrating if you were expecting to be sitting next to your colleague.

—I understand that the discussion is very important to you.

3. Solutions

—I will look around the cabin to see if there are two vacant seats together.

—Thank you very much for your feedback, Mr. Freeman. We do appreciate your comments.

4. Assurance of service

—If there is anything we can do for you, please don't hesitate to let us know.

3.3 Case Analysis: The Service on This Flight Is Terrible! (个案分析：这个飞机上的服务太糟糕了！)

How would you like to deal with the following condition?

Passenger: The service on this flight is terrible. The dinner service was very rushed and none of the crew smiled once. I may as well be in economy class!

1. Acknowledgement

Mr. Paul, please accept my apologies. I am sorry to hear that our service is not up to standard.

2. Empathy

—I can understand that you feel quite disappointed about the service.

—I can feel that you are very upset about the service.

3. Options/Alternatives

—May I ask if there is anything else you would care to try?

—Would you care for another...?

4. Thank passengers for their feedback

—I appreciate your comments regarding the service today.

—Thank you very much for taking the time to share your concerns for the service today. We do appreciate your feedback.

5. Assurance of service

—Mr. Paul, if there is anything else we can do for you, please do not hesitate to let us know.

6. Follow up service

—Excuse me, we will be starting our breakfast service shortly. May I reserve the meal for you first?

Words and Expressions

mindset [ˈmaɪndset] *n.* 心态；倾向；习惯；精神状态；思维模式；思想倾向

priority [praɪˈɒrɪtɪ] *n.* 优先权；优先处理的事

unfair [ˌʌnˈfeə] *adj.* 不公平的，不公正的

criticism [ˈkrɪtɪsɪzəm] *n.* 批评，批判；指责；评论

grievance [ˈgri:vəns] *n.* 不满，不平；委屈

temptation [tempˈteɪʃən] *n.* 引诱；诱惑物

objective [əbˈdʒektɪv] *adj.* 客观的；客观存在的，真实的

wording [ˈwɜ:dɪŋ] *n.* 措辞；用语

subtly [ˈsʌtli] *adv.* 精细地；巧妙地；敏锐地

partnership [ˈpɑ:tnəʃɪp] *n.* 合伙；合伙企业；合作关系

resist [rɪˈzɪst] *vt.* 抵抗；忍耐，忍住

rightly [ˈraɪtlɪ] *adv.* 正确地；有道理的

option [ˈɒpʃən] *n.* 选择权；买卖的特权；[计]选项

Conversations on Board Part II

assurance [əˈʃʊərəns] *n.* 保证，担保；(人寿)保险；自信
resolution [ˌrezəˈluːʃən] *n.* 决议；解决；决心
expectation [ˌekspekˈteɪʃən] *n.* 期待；预期；指望
grace [greɪs] *n.* 优雅；高雅；体面
tension [ˈtenʃən] *n.* 张力，拉力；紧张，焦虑

Practice

How would you like to deal with the following condition?

Work in groups, and discuss the following issues given to find the solutions. Thereafter each group shares their result with the class, and other groups can supplement with new ideas. Play the roles of the flight attendant and the passenger respectively.

1. You are supposed to be a flight attendant, and a passenger was complaining loudly, "The food on this flight is disgusting! I should have taken another flight!"

2. You are supposed to be a flight attendant. A man complains he hasn't been served any drinks. The fact is that he was sleeping while you served. How would you like to explain to him?

3. You are supposed to be a flight attendant. A lady asks for hot drinks but there are no hot drinks on board because the water system is out of order. How would you like to explain to her?

Unit 4   Communication with Passengers

(与乘客沟通)

Directions: Translate the English sentences on the left into Chinese, check your answer in the right column, and then interpret the Chinese text into English while reading.

4.1 Boarding(登机)

4.1.1 Greetings(欢迎)

1. Good morning(afternoon/evening)! Welcome aboard Air China!	1. 您好！欢迎您乘坐国航航班！
2. Welcome aboard Air China, a member of Star Alliance!	2. 您好，欢迎您乘坐星空联盟成员国航航班！
3. Good morning(afternoon/evening). May I have a look at your boarding pass?	3. 早上(下午/晚上)好！我能看一下您的登机牌吗？
4. Mr./Ms. _____, may I offer you the hot towel?	4. _____先生/女士，我可以向您提供热毛巾吗？
5. Mr./Ms. _____, we have prepared orange juice, mineral water and champagne for you. Which one would you like?	5. _____先生/女士，我们为您准备了橙汁、矿泉水和香槟酒，请问您喜欢哪一种？
6. Mr./Ms. _____, would you like to put on slippers? It will make you more comfortable.	6. _____先生/女士，您需要换一下拖鞋吗？这样会舒服些。
7. Mr./Ms. _____, would you like to try the champagne? We've got Cartier.	7. _____先生/女士，需要品尝一下香槟吗？我们配备的是卡迪亚香槟。
8. It's quite cold. Would you like a cup of hot tea?	8. 天气比较冷，您需要一杯热茶吗？

4.1.2 Seating(座位)

1. Good morning(afternoon/evening)! This way (aisle), please.

2. Good morning(afternoon/evening)! Mr./Ms. _____. Business class is in upper deck. Please go this way.

3. Seat numbers are indicated on the overhead compartments.

4. Your seat number is 20D. Please follow me.

5. Excuse me. Please give way to the passengers behind.

6. Sure. I'll see if there is any vacant seat for you in the first row after boarding.

7. 25E is vacant. You can change there after take-off.

8. Excuse me. The lady next to you wants to sit together with her child. Would you mind changing seats with her?

9. Excuse me. I have talked with that passenger, but he still preferred the window seat.

10. I am afraid we cannot upgrade you on board. May I suggest you arrange that procedure in advance at check-in counter next time?

11. Excuse me, sir, this is the crew seat. May I kindly ask you to return to your original seat? Thank you for your cooperation.

12. In order to keep the aircraft in balance, please return to your original seat. Thank you.

13. I am sorry. Please take a seat first. I will check it with the ground staff and be back soon.

14. Thank you for waiting. It is our fault. Your seat number is 15B. I'll show you the way.

1. 早上(下午/晚上)好！请从这边(通道)往前走。

2. 早上(下午/晚上)好！_____先生/女士，请从这边上楼梯，楼上是公务舱。

3. 座椅排号在行李架上方。

4. 您的座位是 20 排 D 座，请跟我来。

5. 麻烦您侧一下身，让后面的旅客过去。

6. 好的，旅客登机完毕后，我帮您看看第一排有没有空座位。

7. 25E 座位没有旅客，起飞后您可以去坐。

8. 对不起，您旁边的旅客想和她的孩子坐在一起。您方便跟她换一下座位吗？

9. 对不起，我已沟通过了，但那位旅客还是想坐靠窗的座位。

10. 对不起，机上无法办理升舱手续。建议您下次在地面提前办理。

11. 对不起，先生，这里是机组座位。我可以请您回到您原来的座位吗？谢谢您的合作！

12. 为了使飞机保持配载平衡，请您回到原来的座位坐好，谢谢您的合作。

13. 很抱歉。请先坐下。我请地服人员查询一下，马上就回来。

14. 让您久等了，这是我们工作的失误。您现在可以坐在 15 排 B 座，我带您过去。

Conversations on Board Part II

15. Sir/Madam, the seat you are taking is in emergency exit area. You are kindly requested to read the safety instruction and not to touch the red handle. We do appreciate your help in case of emergency.

15. 先生/女士，您坐的是应急出口的位置，这是说明书，请您看一下，红色手柄不能触碰，在紧急情况下，请您协助我们的工作。

4.1.3 Belongings(随身物品)

1. I am afraid your baggage is too big to go into the overhead compartment. May I help you check it in?

2. Could you take your passport, the valuables, or the fragile items out of your luggage?

3. Sir/Madam, is this your luggage? Could you put it under the seat in front of you or into the overhead compartment?

4. Sir, I do apologize that there is no space in the overhead locker above your seat. I understand you would like to keep your bag close to you. May I suggest you stow it under the seat in front of you?

5. Sir/Madam, is this your baggage? This is the emergency exit. For your safety, you are kindly requested to put it into the overhead compartment.

6. Mr./Ms. _____, May I help you hang up your coat in the closet?

7. Sir, could you remove all valuable items and important documents from your pockets? May I have your boarding pass as well? We will return your clothes before landing. Is that all right for you?

1. 您的行李太大，行李架里放不下。我帮您托运吧？

2. 您能取出您行李中的护照、贵重及易碎物品吗？

3. 先生/女士，这是您的行李吗？您可以把它放在您前方的座椅下面，或者放在行李架上吗？

4. 先生，我很抱歉，您座椅上方的行李架没地方了。我明白您想把包放在身边。我建议您把它放在您前方座椅的下面，好吗？

5. 先生/女士，请问这是您的行李吗？这是应急出口。为了您的安全，请您把它放在行李架上。

6. _____先生/女士，我能帮您把衣服挂在衣帽间吗？

7. 先生，您能把贵重物品和重要证件从口袋里取出吗？请给我您的登机牌好吗？落地前我们会归还您的衣服。您看这样行吗？

Words and Expressions

regular [ˈregjələ] *adj.* 有规律的；规则的；标准大小的

process [ˈprəʊses] *n.* 过程；工序，工艺流程；变化过程

towel [ˈtaʊəl] *n.* 毛巾；抹布

overhead [ˌəʊvəˈhed] *adv.* 在头顶上方；在空中

take-off [ˈteɪkɔːf] *n.* 起飞

upgrade [ʌpˈgreɪd] *vt.* 提高(飞机乘客、旅馆住客等的)待遇；使(机器、计算机系统等)升级；提高(设施、服务等的)档次

arrange [əˈreɪndʒ] *vt.* 安排，筹划；整理，排列

procedure [prəˈsiːdʒə] *n.* 程序，手续；步骤

in advance 预先，事先；提前

check-in counter 办理登机手续柜台

cooperation [kəʊˌɒpəˈreɪʃən] *n.* 合作，协作；配合

original [əˈrɪdʒənl] *adj.* 原始的；独创的；最初的

fault [fɔːlt] *n.* 缺点，缺陷；过错，责任

instruction [ɪnˈstrʌkʃn] *n.* 用法说明；操作指南；指令；教导，指导

handle [ˈhændl] *n.* (门上的)拉手，把手

appreciate [əˈpriːʃieɪt] *vt.* 感激；欣赏；领会，理解

belongings [bɪˈlɒŋɪŋz] *n.* 所有物；财产，财物

compartment [kəmˈpɑːtmənt] *n.* 隔间(尤指火车车厢中的)；隔层

check up 调查，检查；清理

valuables [ˈvæljuəblz] *n.* (尤指珠宝等)贵重物品

fragile [ˈfrædʒaɪl] *adj.* 易碎的，脆的；虚弱的

luggage [ˈlʌgɪdʒ] *n.* 行李

locker [ˈlɒkə] *n.* 寄物柜；冷藏间

hang up 挂上；挂起；将电话筒挂上，挂断电话

document [ˈdɒkjumənt] *n.* (计算机中的)文档，文件；公文

vacant [ˈveɪkənt] *adj.* 空闲的；空缺的；空虚的

apologize [əˈpɒlədʒaɪz] *vi.* 道歉，认错

boarding pass 登机牌

Conversations on Board Part II

4.2 Before Take-off(起飞前)

4.2.1 Safety Check(安全检查)

1. Please fasten your seat belt and put your seat back upright.

2. Sir/Madam, our plane is taxiing. Please switch off your mobile phone.

3. Sir/Madam, as we are taking off shortly, for your safety, please return to your seat and fasten seat belt.

4. As we are taking off shortly, it's dangerous to leave your seat. Could you remain seated until we get to the cruising level?

5. Excuse me, sir. According to the CAAC regulations, all mobile phones including those with flight mode must be switched off throughout the flight. Thank you for your cooperation.

6. Sir, I understand that this phone call is very important for you. However, for your safety, please ensure that your mobile phone is switched off now.

7. As we are taking off soon, please put your seat back upright, secure your tray-table and footrest.

8. As we're taking off soon, for your safety, please make sure your window shades are drawn up (so that we can see what is happening outside in case of emergency).

---

1. 请系好安全带，将座椅靠背调直。

2. 先生/女士，我们的飞机正在滑行，请关闭您的手机。

3. 先生/女士，我们的飞机马上就要起飞了，为了您的安全，请您马上回到座位上坐好并系好安全带。

4. 由于我们的飞机马上就要起飞了，这时离开您的座位是危险的。请在飞机平飞之后离开座位好吗？

5. 对不起，先生。根据中国民航相关规定，所有手机包括有飞行模式的手机都需要全程关闭。感谢您的配合。

6. 先生，我知道这个电话对您非常重要。但是，为了您的安全，请确保您的手机已关闭。

7. 我们的飞机马上就要起飞了，请您调直座椅靠背，收起小桌板和脚踏板。

8. 我们很快就要起飞了，为了您的安全，请把遮光板打开(这样我们随时可以在紧急情况下看到外面发生了什么)。

4.2.2　Cabin Getting Ready(客舱准备)

1. The aircraft is taking off immediately. May I serve you right after take-off?

2. Mr./Ms. _____, the aircraft is taking off immediately. May I help you stow your personal video?

3. Cabin attendants, please return to your seats for takeoff/landing.

1. 飞机马上就要起飞了，起飞后我再为您服务，好吗？

2. _____先生/女士，飞机马上要起飞了，我能帮您把小屏幕收起来吗？

3. 飞机马上就要起飞/落地，请乘务员回座位坐好。

Words and Expressions

safety check　安全检查

seat belt　安全带

taxi [ˈtæksi] *vi.* (飞机起飞前或着陆后)滑行

cruise [kru:z] *vi.* 乘船游览；(汽车、飞机等)以平稳的速度行驶

switch [swɪtʃ] *vt. & vi.* 转变，开关；转换

compliance [kəmˈplaɪəns] *n.* 遵守；服从，听从

CAAC *abbr.* (Civil Aviation Administration of China)　中国民用航空总局

regulation [ˌregjuˈleɪʃn] *n.* 管理；控制；规章；规则

cabin [ˈkæbɪn] *n.* 小木屋；客舱；(轮船上工作或生活的)隔间

4.3　In-flight Service(空中服务)

4.3.1　General(常规的)

1. What can I do for you?/How may I help you?

1. 我能为您做些什么吗？我可以帮您吗？

Conversations on Board Part II

2. Mr./Ms. _____, today you are taking our luxurious first class named Forbidden Pavilion (Business class named Capital Pavilion). I'm _____. I'm glad to be at your service. If you need any help, please do not hesitate to call me.

3. The flight time today is ten hours and twenty-five minutes.

4. E-ticket will be put into use from the 1st of June in Air China. You can easily book tickets and print boarding pass online.

5. It is my pleasure/great honor to be at your service.

6. We are pleased to answer your questions.

7. The different color uniforms represent different ranks of flight attendants.

8. I am sorry, I am not sure. Let me check with my colleagues.

9. I am sorry, I am not sure of our exact location. May I refer you to the air show on the PTV?

10. On behalf of the entire crew, I'd like to say happy birthday to you.

11. This is the call button. Please press it if you need any help.

12. The aircraft you are taking is a Boeing 747/Airbus 340.

13. The lavatory is in the front/center/rear of the aircraft. Please follow me.

14. Hope you will have a nice stay in Beijing.

15. I hope this trip to Beijing will leave you happy memories.

16. The next Olympic Games will be held in Tokyo.

17. Whether win or not, the athletes have done their utmost/best.

18. Badminton is a fascinating sport.

19. With this climate of the season, it's suitable to tour around Beijing.

20. How long are you going to stay in Beijing?

21. How long have you been in China?

2. _____先生/女士，您今天乘坐的是豪华紫金头等舱(紫宸公务舱)。我是_____，很高兴能为您服务。如果有什么需要，请毫不犹豫地叫我。

3. 今天的飞行时间是10小时25分。

4. 国航将从6月1日起使用电子客票，您可以从网上直接购票和办理登机牌。

5. 为您服务是我的荣幸。

6. 我们很乐意回答您的问题。

7. 不同颜色的制服代表乘务员的不同级别。

8. 对不起，我不是很清楚，我问一下我的同事。

9. 对不起，我不太清楚我们的确切位置。请您查看个人电视上的航路信息好吗？

10. 我谨代表全体机组成员祝您生日快乐。

11. 这是呼叫铃，需要帮助时您可以按下这个按钮。

12. 您今天乘坐的是波音747/空客340飞机。

13. 卫生间在飞机的前部/中部/后部。请您跟我来。

14. 希望您在北京过得愉快。

15. 希望这次北京之行能给您留下美好的回忆。

16. 下一届奥运会将在东京举行。

17. 无论输赢，运动员们都尽了最大努力。

18. 羽毛球比赛是一项很吸引人的运动。

19. 北京现在的气候非常适合旅游。

20. 您打算在北京停留多久呢？

21. 您来中国多久了？

4.3.2　Safety(安全)

1. I understand it's tiring for such a long flight. You can move around in the cabin. However, for your safety, I suggest you not stay long at the emergency exit.

2. Excuse me, sir. It is not safe lying on the floor. It might bruise you in case of turbulence and threaten others. Please be seated and fasten your seat belt.

3. Because of turbulence, please return to your seats and fasten your seat belts. For your safety, toilets should not be used at this time.

4. The fasten seat belt sign is off now. You may use the lavatories at the center or the rear of the cabin.

5. Please stow your tray-table as soon as you finish filling in the form.

6. For your safety, the lavatories have to be closed prior to landing. Please refrain from using it until the plane lands and comes to a complete stop.

1. 航线很长，如果您感到疲倦，可以在客舱里稍微活动一下。但这里是紧急出口，为了安全请您不要长时间在此停留。

2. 对不起，先生。在地板上休息很危险，飞机颠簸时会伤到您，并对其他旅客造成威胁。请您回到座位上系好安全带。

3. 飞机现在遇到不稳定气流，请您回原位坐好并系好安全带。为了您的安全，卫生间暂时停止使用。

4. 安全带信号已经解除，您可使用客舱中部或后部的洗手间。

5. 请您填好表格后把小桌板收起来。

6. 为了您的安全，在着陆前我们将关闭卫生间。请等到飞机完全停稳后再使用。

4.3.3　Beverages(饮料)

1. Mr. _____, it is time for afternoon tea. We have prepared various tea and refreshments for you to enjoy the leisure on board.

2. Mr./Ms. _____, we have Oolong tea, Longjing tea, Black tea, Chrysanthemum tea, Steamed tea, Jasmine tea and Green tea. Which one would you like?

3. Mr./Ms. _____, how would you like your tea, weak or strong?

1. _____先生，现在是下午茶时间，我们准备了各种茶点，希望您在飞机上能够享受一份悠闲。

2. _____先生/女士，我们有乌龙茶、龙井茶、红茶、菊花茶、煎茶、茉莉花茶、绿茶，您喜欢哪一种？

3. _____先生/女士，您喜欢淡茶还是浓茶？

Conversations on Board Part II

4. Mr./Ms. _____, it is spring, so we suggest you drink Jasmine tea which is rich in various vitamins and (hence) proved to be a sobering pick-me-up.

5. Mr./Ms. _____, do you need any rock candy in Chrysanthemum tea?

6. It seems the tea is getting cold. Let me make a new one for you.

7. It's good to separate the tea-leaf from water when drinking colong tea. Soaking in the water for a long time will destroy its taste.

8. Here is your coffe/tea/hot water. Be cautious when holding it. It is quite hot.

9. We have prepared various kinds of tea, coffee, juice, carbonated drinks, mineral water, and alcoholic drinks like red wine, brandy, whisky, gin and vodka. Which one would you like?

10. Mr./Ms. _____, we have red wine, white wine, Cognac, Whisky, Gin, Vodka. Which one would you like?

11. How should I prepare your cocktail, sir?

12. Would you like a glass of red wine? And how about a glass of water as well?

13. Would you like a cup of coffee? We have Nestle golden coffee and cappuccino.

14. Mr./Ms. _____, we have lots of choices for red wine such as French Legende Bordeaux, Bordeaux d'Estournel, American Silver Stone and Chinese Great Wall Cabernet Sauvignon. Which one would you like?

15. May I put your drink on the table, so as not to spill it on your computer?

16. We didn't disturb you when you were having a rest. Would you like something to drink now? We have juice, carbonated drinks, mineral water, hot tea and coffee. Which one would you like?

17. Madam, I do apologize that pineapple juice is not available on this flight. May I offer you orange juice or apple juice instead?

18. I am afraid wine is not available. May I offer you beer instead?

19. May I take the glass away?

4. _____先生/女士，现在是春天，建议您喝茉莉花茶，它富含维生素，能提神醒脑。

5. _____先生/女士，菊花茶里需要加冰糖吗？

6. 茶水好像凉了，让我为您换一杯新泡的吧。

7. 乌龙茶适宜沥干后饮用，最好不长时间在水里浸泡。

8. 这是您的咖啡/茶/热水。小心烫，请拿好。

9. 我们准备了各种茶、咖啡、果汁、碳酸饮料、矿泉水以及酒精饮料，如红酒、白兰地、威士忌、杜松子、伏特加。请问您喜欢哪一种？

10. _____先生/女士，我们有红葡萄酒、科尼亚克白兰地、威士忌、杜松子、伏特加，请问您喜欢哪一种？

11. 先生，请问如何调制您的鸡尾酒？

12. 请问您需要喝杯红酒吗？再给您倒一杯水怎么样？

13. 请问您需要咖啡吗？我们有雀巢金牌咖啡和卡布奇诺咖啡。

14. _____先生/女士，红葡萄酒有法国拉菲传奇波尔多、埃斯杜那儿波尔多、美国银矿干红、中国长城赤霞珠红酒，请问您喜欢哪一种？

15. 我能帮您把饮料放在小桌板上吗，以免洒在电脑上？

16. 刚才您在休息，我没有打扰您。请问您要喝点饮料吗？我们有果汁、碳酸饮料、矿泉水，还有热茶和咖啡，您喜欢哪种？

17. 对不起，女士，我们的飞机上没有菠萝汁，我向您推荐橙汁或苹果汁，好吗？

18. 对不起，没有葡萄酒。给您啤酒，好吗？

19. 我能帮您把不用的杯子收走吗？

4.3.4　Meals(供餐)

1. Mr./Ms. _____, here's the menu and wine list. We'll take your order soon.

2. Mr./Ms. _____, today we have two meals for you. When would you like to take them? How about 12:00 for lunch service?

3. Mr./Ms. _____, it's 6:00 now. Shall we serve dinner for you?

4. Mr./Ms. _____, may I set the table for you?

5. Mr. _____, the elements of the doors at "the Forbidden City" have been introduced into the design of the new tableware for Forbidden Pavilion first class.

6. Here is the Quan Jude roast duck. You can have it with the slice pancake, soy sauce and cucumber.

7. Mr./Ms. _____, here is the vegetable salad, and we have Thousand Island dressing(a little bit sweet) and Italian Balsamic dressing(a little sour). Which one would you prefer? Would you like some more?

8. Mr./Ms. _____, we also have pickled vegetables and chili sauce. Would you like some of them?

9. Mr. _____, this is the new fashioned tableware for Air China's Forbidden Pavilion first class. The idea is mainly from "the Forbidden City" in Beijing.

10. For the main course of lunch, we have Beijing roast duck, fried fish, Manchurian lamb and beefsteak. Which one would you like?

11. Let me make up your seat while you're away. When you come back, we'll be ready to serve dinner.

12. Let me help you prepare the table.

1. _____先生/女士，这是今天的餐谱和酒单，稍候我们将为您订餐。

2. _____先生/女士，今天为您准备了两顿正餐，您看什么时候用餐？午餐的提供时间在 12 点，可以吗？

3. _____先生/女士，现在是 6 点钟，现在为您开餐可以吗？

4. _____先生/女士，我可以帮您摆一下餐具吗？

5. _____先生，紫金头等舱新餐具的设计引入了"紫禁城"门的要素。

6. 这是全聚德烤鸭，饼、酱、黄瓜可以和烤鸭一起配着吃。

7. _____先生/女士，这是蔬菜沙拉，我们配有千岛汁(味道微甜)和意大利香醋汁(味道偏酸)，请问您喜欢哪种口味？要不要再加一些？

8. _____先生/女士，这是我们为您准备的榨菜和辣酱，要不要尝试一下？

9. _____先生，这是国航紫金头等舱推出的新款餐具，这款餐具的主要概念来源于北京的"紫禁城"。

10. 午餐的主菜有北京烤鸭、煎鱼、八旗羊肉和煎牛扒，您喜欢哪一种？

11. 您离开一下，我来帮您把座位整理一下。等您回来就座，马上为您提供晚餐。

12. 我帮您打开小桌板吧！

Conversations on Board Part II

13. Here is the menu. On today's flight, we have prepared a lunch and a dinner rich in variety and nutrition.

14. Here is the menu. The flight takes about 2 hours, and we will be serving lunch after take-off. There are three options for the main course on this page. Please have a look at the menu first, and I will take your order later.

15. In order to make you feel more at ease, you may have flexible dinner time at 20 minutes after take-off or one and a half hours before landing. We've prepared pan-fried cod fish, Wuxi pork spare ribs and Beijing roast duck.

16. Please don't worry. We will try to meet your need. However, please reserve the special meal next time you book a ticket and confirm it 24 hours before flight.

17. Here is the meal (Child meal, Diabetic meal, Moslem meal, Kosher meal) you ordered.

18. We have prepared fish ball with rice and beef with rice. Which one would you prefer?

19. Here is the meal/hot drink. Be careful.

20. I am very sorry. Beijing roast duck is not available. However, may I suggest today's Wuxi pork spare ribs and beef steak which also taste delicious? Would you like to try them?

21. I am sorry that there is no extra meal today. Is it all right that I bring you some bread or peanuts?

22. If you don't need the main course, how about some fruit?

23. Thank you for your understanding. You will have priority to make a choice for the next meal.

24. For the second meal, which choice would you like to take? I'll reserve it for you.

13. 这是今天航班的餐谱，我们为您准备了品种多样、营养丰富的中餐和晚餐。

14. 这是今天的餐谱，今天的航班大约飞行两个小时，起飞后我们为您提供午餐。主菜有三种，在这一页，您可以先看一下，稍后我帮您订餐。

15. 为了给您创造良好的休息环境，您可以选择在起飞后 20 分钟或下降前一个半小时用餐。我们今天为您精心准备了香煎鳕鱼、无锡排骨和北京烤鸭。

16. 您别担心，我们会尽力满足您的要求。但请您在下次订票时预定特殊的餐食，并于乘机前 24 小时再次确认您的餐食。

17. 这是您预订的餐食(儿童餐、糖尿病餐、穆斯林餐、犹太餐)。

18. 今天我们为您准备了鱼丸米饭和牛肉米饭，请问您喜欢哪一种？

19. 这是您的餐食/热饮，小心烫手！

20. 实在抱歉，北京烤鸭没有了。不过，今天的无锡排骨和牛排的味道也不错，您愿意试试吗？

21. 很抱歉，今天的餐食没有多余的了，我帮您找一些面包或花生好吗？

22. 您若是不需要主菜了，那么来点水果如何？(客人不用主菜时)

23. 感谢您的理解，下一餐我们一定请您优先选择。

24. 对于第二顿餐食您喜欢哪种？我会为您留着。

25. We also offer snacks(biscuits/sandwiches) between meals.

26. We will be showing an exercise video soon. Dinner will be served right after that.

27. Here is the Italian Balsamic dressing. Would you like some more?

28. Good appetite.

29. May I get you a new set of cutlery?

30. Thank you for waiting. Here is the Beijing Quan Jude roast duck. Hope you like it.

31. We have seafood with fried rice and chicken with fried noodles. The fried noodles are really delicious. Would you like to taste it?

32. Well, let me check for you. I will bring it over if there is an extra.

33. Madam, I apologize that you are not happy with your meal. We are also serving sweet and sour chicken on steamed rice. Would you care/like to taste it?

34. Sir, I understand you are feeling frustrated because your vegetarian meal is not available on the flight. I fully appreciate how important the special meal is for you. I will do my best to arrange an alternative vegetarian meal for you.

35. No problem, I will take away your tray in a minute.

36. Is the meal we prepared for you good today?

37. Sorry. The dishware is not disposable. It can be cleaned, sterilized and reused.

38. Would you like some more bread?

39. Mr. _____, how do you like the meal?

40. I am glad that you love Chinese cuisine.

25. 两餐之间，我们还会提供小吃(饼干或三明治)。

26. 稍后我们将播放健身操。健身操后，我们将为您提供晚餐。

27. 这是您选的意大利香醋汁。您需要再加点吗?

28. 祝您用餐愉快。

29. 我能为您更换一套新餐具吗?

30. 让您久等了。这是您订的全聚德烤鸭。希望您能喜欢。

31. 我们为您准备了海鲜炒饭和鸡肉炒面。今天的炒面做得不错，您想尝尝吗?

32. 好的，我去帮您看一下。如果有多余的我会帮您拿过来。(旅客想再要一份餐食的时候)

33. 很抱歉，女士，您对您的餐食不满意。我们还有咕咾鸡肉盖饭，您想尝一下吗?

34. 先生，我理解您很不满飞机上没有您预订的素食，我能体会到这个特殊餐食对您有多么重要。我会尽我所能给您准备一份素食替代。

35. 没问题，我马上收走您的餐盘。

36. 我们今天为您准备的餐食还可口吗?

37. 抱歉，我们的餐具不是一次性用品。清洁消毒后可以再次利用。

38. 您还需要再加一些面包吗?

39. _____先生，您喜欢这顿餐吗?

40. 我很高兴您喜欢中国美食。

Conversations on Board

4.3.5 Duty Free Sales(免税品销售)

1. Mr./Ms. _____, here is the shopping guide. Please tell the flight attendant if you need any help.

2. You can order the duty-free items on the shopping list, and then give it to the flight attendant.

3. You'd better read the shopping guide carefully before making the purchase. If you like, we can recommend some items suitable for you.

4. Would you like to pay by cash or credit card?

5. We accept cash (RMB, US dollar, euro, pound) and credit card (Diner's Club, Master, Visa and American Express).

6. If you pay by the credit card, we may need your passport as well.

7. Have you got any small change?

8. Here is your change. Please check it up.

9. This credit card has expired. Would you please pay in other ways or by another card?

10. I'm afraid only some of the duty-free items have discount during sales promotion.

11. If you like, I may recommend some duty-free items for you.

12. The color of this lipstick(the fragrance of the perfume /the bracelet) is quite fit for a young lady like you.

13. The perfume you want is sold out. How about other brands? They are also of good quality.

1. _____先生/女士，这是购物介绍单，如果您需要什么商品可以随时告诉乘务员。

2. 您可订购购物单上的免税商品，选中所需商品后交给乘务员。

3. 请您在购买免税商品之前，一定要仔细阅读商品介绍单。如果您需要我们的帮助，我可以先向您推荐几款适合您的商品。

4. 请问您是用现金还是用信用卡支付？

5. 我们可以收取现金(人民币、美元、欧元、英镑等) 和信用卡(大莱卡、万事达、维萨、美国运通卡等)。

6. 如果您使用信用卡付款，我们还需要您的护照。

7. 请问您有零钱吗？

8. 这是找给您的钱，请点清、拿好！

9. 这张信用卡已经过期了。您能用其他的付款方式或者换另外一张信用卡吗？

10. 真不好意思，我们只有在促销活动期间部分免税商品可以打折。

11. 如果您需要，我可以向您推荐几款适合您的免税商品。

12. 这款口红的颜色(香水味道/手镯)非常适合像您这样的年轻女性。

13. 您想要的香水已卖完。其他品牌的怎么样呢？它们的品质也很好。

14. You can reserve duty-free items on our official website www.airchina.com.cn.

15. Here are the duty-free items you have bought. Please check them up.

16. If you are on transit, please put the liquid items you have bought on board into this transparent plastic bag, keep it sealed and have the boarding pass ready when going through the security check.

17. Here is the Olympic badge on sale. It's a nice souvenir.

14. 您可以从国航官方网站 www.airchina.com.cn 上预定您喜欢的免税商品。

15. 这是您购买的免税商品。请您核对一下。

16. 如果您需要转机，在飞机上购买的液体免税品请放在这个透明的塑料袋内，保持封口。通过安检时，需要您出示这段航程的登机牌，以备查验。

17. 这是我们飞机上出售的奥运徽章，很有纪念价值。

4.3.6　Phoenix Miles and Change for Hope(知音卡和零钱捐赠)

1. Mr. _____, would you like an application form for Phoenix Miles membership? To apply, please fill in the form and give it together with your boarding pass to a cabin attendant.

2. Please make sure your address and telephone number are accurate.

3. Please accumulate your miles at the check-in counter.

4. The money raised in the donation activity will be spent on building the "Project Hope Physical Training Playground" to outfit athletic facilities for needy children.

5. You can put some change into this envelope, keep it sealed and give it to the cabin attendants.

1. _____先生，请问您需要国航知音入会申请表吗？填写完表格后和登机牌一起交给乘务员就可以申请办理了。

2. 请确认您的地址和电话号码准确无误。

3. 请您在办理登机牌的柜台登记积累您的里程。

4. 零钱捐赠活动的善款将用于援建"希望工程快乐体育园地"，为需要帮助的孩子们配置体育设施。

5. 您可以把零钱放在这个信封里，密封后交给乘务员。

4.3.7 Air Bar(空中酒廊)

1. The cocktails and mixed drinks served in Air Bar are all invented by the flight attendants. Would you like to try them?

2. Mr./Ms. _____, would you like a glass of cocktail? It has a pretty color and rich taste.

3. The Dream of Jiangnan has a pretty color and good taste. It's nice to drink in summer. I hope you'll like it.

4. The Dancing Phoenix with Auspicious Cloud is alcohol free. It is quite suitable for ladies.

5. The main ingredients of the Dancing Phoenix with Auspicious Cloud are black tea and sprite. It tastes very good.

6. The Dancing in Golden Autumn are Gin and Chrysanthemum tea. The taste is fresh with a touch of bitterness.

7. The Dancing in Golden Autumn can be served either with or without sugar. Which would you prefer?

1. 空中酒廊的饮品都是由乘务员自行调制的。请问您要试一试吗？

2. _____先生/女士，请问您需要喝一杯鸡尾酒吗？这杯酒调出来的颜色非常漂亮，口感也特别好！

3. 这款梦幻江南色泽诱人，口感也很好，非常适合夏季饮用。希望您能喜欢。

4. 这款凤舞祥云不含酒精，非常适合女士饮用。

5. 凤舞祥云主要成分是红茶和雪碧，口味甜美。

6. 金秋之舞主要成分是杜松子酒和菊花茶，口感略清苦。

7. 金秋之舞有含糖和不含糖两种。请问您需要哪种？

4.3.8 CIQ(海关移民局检疫)

1. Here are the customs declaration form and entry card. You may fill out the forms in Chinese or English and keep them together with your passport. It'll be convenient for you to go through the entry formalities in the terminal building.

2. Here is the entry card. You may fill it out before landing and submit it to the immigration officers.

1. 这是您的海关申报单和入境卡。您可以用中文或英文填写表格，并将其和您的护照放在一起，可以方便您在到达候机楼时办理入境手续。

2. 这是入境卡。您可以在落地前填好，落地后交给移民局官员。

3. For the customs declaration form of the United States, only one form is required for a family traveling together.

4. Please use capital letters to fill in the entry card and customs declaration form of the United States.

5. Finally, please make sure to sign your name.

6. You are required to show these forms to the officers when going through immigration, customs and quarantine procedures.

7. Chinese Customs permits 2 cartons of cigarette into the country, so you'd better not exceed the limit.

8. According to the quarantine requirements of the local government, passengers are not allowed to bring fresh fruits into the country.

9. Please complete these forms before arriving in Shanghai and keep it together with your passport.

3. 美国海关申报单，一个家庭可填写一份。

4. 请用英文大写字母填写美国入境卡和申报单。

5. 最后，请确认签上您的名字。

6. 当您办理入境、海关和检疫等手续时需要出示这些表格。

7. 中国的海关规定只允许旅客携带两条香烟入境，您最好不要携带超过这个数目的香烟。

8. 根据当地检疫规定，乘客不能携带新鲜水果入境。

9. 请您在到达上海之前填写好这些表格，并将其和您的护照放在一起。

4.3.9　Relaxation(娱乐休息)

1. Sir/Madam, may I turn on the reading light for you?

2. Mr./Ms. ＿＿＿＿, here's the newspaper prepared for you. We have *Xinjing Newspaper*, *Beijing Evening*, *Economics Daily*, *People's Daily*, *Global Times*, *Life Weekly*, *Beijing Youth*. We hope you'll like them.

3. Mr./Ms. ＿＿＿＿, do you need a blanket? Would you like me to put it on for you?

1. 先生/女士，需要我为您打开阅读灯吗？

2. ＿＿＿＿先生/女士，这是我们为您准备的报纸，有新京报、北京晚报、经济日报、人民日报、环球时报、生活周刊、北京青年报，希望您喜欢。

3. ＿＿＿＿先生/女士，您需要毛毯吗？您需要我帮您盖上吗？

Conversations on Board Part II

4. Mr. _____, may I close the window shade so that the bright sunlight won't disturb you?

5. Excuse me, Mr./ Ms. _____. Here's the entertainment system guide/seat instruction. If you have any questions, do let me know. I'll be more than happy to help you (We are pleased to answer all questions at all times).

6. Mr./Ms. _____, the movies we have on board include comedy, action movies and features. _____ is the latest released movie. Here's the entertainment guide. Enjoy your time.

7. Sir, our in-flight entertainment details are available in the *Wings of China* magazine, which is located in the seat pocket in front of you.

8. Mr. _____, may I help you adjust the seat to a more comfortable position, so that you can have a good rest?

9. Folk songs, classic music, pop music and Chinese opera will be available in our in-flight audio system. You can choose what you like.

10. Please push the button on the armrest and lean against the seat back at the same time.

11. You may close the sun shade board (sun shield/window shade) and turn off the reading light when sleeping. But don't forget to fasten your seat belt.

12. The headset socket is in the armrest. You may enjoy the audio programs at your preference by selecting channels.

13. The movie audio is usually on channel 1 or 2.

4. _____先生，我能帮您拉下遮光板吗？以免干扰您休息。

5. _____先生/女士，打扰您了。这是娱乐系统指南/座椅使用说明。如果您有疑问，请随时找我。我将非常高兴为您提供帮助(我们很乐意随时解答您的疑问)。

6. _____先生/女士，今天我们为您准备的影片有：喜剧片、动作片、剧情片。_____是最新上映的影片。这是娱乐指南，请您欣赏。

7. 先生，您可以在《中国之翼》杂志上看到我们机上娱乐的详细介绍，杂志就在您前面的座椅口袋里。

8. _____先生，我可以帮您把座椅调整到比较舒适的位置吗？这样您就可以好好休息了。

9. 飞机上的音频系统有民歌、古典音乐、流行音乐和中国戏剧。您可以选择您喜欢的。

10. 您只要按下座椅扶手上的按钮，身体同时往后靠就可以了。

11. 休息时您可以放下遮阳板，关掉阅读灯，但请系好您的安全带。

12. 耳机插孔在座椅扶手上，选择频道后，您就能听到自己喜欢的音乐节目。

13. 电影的音频通常是在1或2频道。

Words and Expressions

forbid [fəˈbɪd] vt. 禁止；阻止
pavilion [pəˈvɪliən] n. 亭，阁楼；(公共活动或展览用的)临时建筑物；大型文体馆；看台
at your service   愿意为您效劳
location [ləʊˈkeɪʃn] n. 位置，场所；定位
on behalf of   为了……的利益；代表……
Tokyo [ˈtəʊkɪəʊ] n. 东京
button [ˈbʌtn] n. 按钮，电钮
airbus [ˈeəbʌs] n. 空中客车(中、短程距离载客用之飞机，也写作 air bus)
utmost [ˈʌtməʊst] adj. 极度的，最大的，最远的
　　　　　　n. 极限，最大限度
turbulence [ˈtɜ:bjələns] n. 骚动，骚乱；[物]湍流；(海洋、天气等的)狂暴；动荡
rear [rɪə] n. 后部，后面；臀部
stow [stəʊ] vt. 装，装载；收藏
lavatory [ˈlævətri] n. 厕所；盥洗室
refrain [rɪˈfreɪn] vt. 抑制，克制
　　　　　　vi. 忍耐，节制
chrysanthemum [krɪˈsænθəməm] n. 菊花；菊属
jasmine [ˈdʒæzmɪn] n. 茉莉；茉莉香料
sober [ˈsəʊbə] vt. & vi. (使)冷静，(使)清醒；使严肃
　　　　　adj. 头脑清醒的；没喝醉的；认真的；朴素的
pick-me-up [ˈpɪkmi:ʌp] n. 含酒精的饮料，提神的酒
rock candy   冰糖
brandy [ˈbrændi] n. 白兰地酒
whisky [ˈwɪski] n. 威士忌酒
gin [dʒɪn] n. 杜松子酒
vodka [ˈvɒdkə] n. 伏特加酒
tableware [ˈteɪblweə(r)] n. 餐具；食具
roast [rəʊst] vt. & vi. 烤，烘，焙
　　　　　n. 烤肉；户外烧烤野餐
　　　　　adj. 烤好的，烤制的
slice [slaɪs] vt. 把……切成薄片
soy sauce   酱；酱油

cucumber [ˈkju:kʌmbə] *n.* 黄瓜

Thousand Island dressing 千岛色拉调味汁

Italian Balsamic dressing 意大利香醋汁

diabetic [ˌdaɪəˈbetɪk] *adj.* 患糖尿病的
　　　　　　　　　　　　n. 糖尿病患者

Moslem [ˈmɒzləm] *n.* 穆斯林，伊斯兰教徒
　　　　　　　　　adj. 穆斯林的

kosher [ˈkəʊʃə] *adj.* (尤指食物)合适的(合乎犹太教教规的)

reserve [rɪˈzɜ:v] *vt.* 保留；预约

alternative [ɔ:lˈtɜ:nətɪv] *adj.* 可替代的；备选的；另类的

disposable [dɪˈspəʊzəbl] *adj.* 一次性的，可任意处理的；用后就抛弃的

sterilize [ˈsterəlaɪz] *vt.* 使消毒；使无菌；使失去生育能力

cuisine [kwɪˈzi:n] *n.* 烹饪，烹调法；菜肴

duty-free [ˈdju:tɪ fri:] *adj.* 免税的，无税的

purchase [ˈpɜ:tʃəs] *v.* 购买；采购
　　　　　　　　　　　n. 购买；购买行为

euro [ˈjʊərəʊ] *n.* 欧元(欧洲经济共同体的统一货币单位)

sterling [ˈstɜ:lɪŋ] *n.* 英国货币

credit card 信用卡

Diner's Club 大来信用卡

Visa card 维萨信用卡

American Express 美国运通卡

expire [ɪkˈspaɪə] *vi.* 文件、协议等到期；期满；失效

perfume [ˈpɜ:fju:m] *n.* 香水；香味，香气

souvenir [ˌsu:vəˈnɪə] *n.* 纪念品；礼物

badge [bædʒ] *n.* 徽章，像章；标记

Phoenix Miles 国航知音卡

application [ˌæplɪˈkeɪʃn] *n.* 申请；申请书，申请表

cabin attendant 客舱乘务员

donation [dəʊˈneɪʃn] *n.* 捐赠，赠送；捐款；捐赠物

athletic [æθˈletɪk] *adj.* 运动的；体格健壮的

declaration [ˌdekləˈreɪʃn] *n.* 宣言，布告，公告，声明；(纳税品在海关的)申报

terminal [ˈtɜ:mɪnl] *n.* 终端；终点站；航空站；航站楼

limousine [ˈlɪməzi:n] *n.* 大型豪华轿车；机场巴士

entry [ˈentri] *n.* 进入权；进入许可；进入；入口处；登记

formality [fɔːˈmæləti] *n.* 正式手续

the Arrival Hall 机场入境大厅

armrest [ˈɑːmrest] *n.* (座位的)靠手，扶手

4.4　Landing(落地)

4.4.1　Disembarkation(下客)

1. The plane is still taxiing along the runway. For your safety, please remain seated.

2. Take your time, please. There will be enough time to collect your items.

3. Please remain seated until the aircraft comes to a complete stop/standstill.

4. Please wait here for a while until the boarding bridge is in position.

5. Thank you, sir. It's so kind of you to make way for this senior gentleman.

6. Please take the transit bus after landing. It will take you directly to the Arrival Hall.

7. Mind/watch your step(Be cautious for the slippery floor, please).

8. Please get your passport ready. The immigration officer will check it when you disembark.

9. Thank you for flying with Air China. We are looking forward to seeing you again.

10. Please make sure to take all your hand luggage and personal belongings when you disembark.

11. Your stroller(pram) has been put at the boarding gate.

12. It is quite cold outside. Please dress warmly before going out.

1. 飞机还在滑行，为了您的安全，请在座位上坐好。

2. 别着急，您有足够的时间整理您的物品。

3. 飞机完全停稳之前，请不要离开座位。

4. 请在这里稍候，您要等到廊桥接好后才能下机。

5. 先生，非常感谢您。您真是太好了，让这位老先生先走。

6. 您到达地面后请乘坐摆渡车，它将直接把您送到进港大厅。

7. 请您小心台阶(小心地滑)。

8. 请将您的护照准备好，下机后有移民局官员进行检查。

9. 感谢您乘坐国航的班机，希望有幸再次为您服务。

10. 下机时请携带好您的手提行李和其他私人物品。

11. 您的婴儿车(手推车)已经放在登机口了。

12. 外面天气冷，请添加随身携带的衣服，以免感冒。

4.4.2 Airport and Destination(机场和目的地)

1. There is a two-hour time difference between Beijing and Sydney. The local time is ten fifteen.

2. The weather in Madrid is colder than that in Beijing. Please put on more coats.

3. Our plane will be parking at Terminal 3. Free transit buses to Terminal 2 are available at Gate 5, on the ground floor.

4. The airport limousine/shuttle bus can take you downtown. The fare is 16 *yuan*.

5. Taxi charges 2 *yuan* per kilometer, and the taxi stand is on the ground floor.

6. It takes about one hour to reach downtown.

7. Our airport inquiry service is 24-hour available. The hotline number is _____.

8. I will write down the hotel's name in Chinese, and then you can show it to the taxi driver. He will take you over there (The charge is about 100 *Yuan*).

9. Which hotel have you reserved?

10. Here is the English version of guidebook for tourists in Beijing/London.

11. I am not quite sure about that. You'd better go to the Information Counter at the terminal building for more information. They will provide assistance.

1. 悉尼与北京的时差是两小时，当地时间是10:15。

2. 马德里的天气比北京冷，请您注意增添一些外套。

3. 我们的飞机将停靠在3号航站楼。您可以在一层5号门乘坐免费摆渡车前往2号航站楼。

4. 机场巴士/摆渡车可带您到达市区。票价是每人16元。

5. 出租车每公里计价为两元。出租车站在一楼。

6. 到达市中心大约需要1个小时。

7. 我们的机场咨询服务24小时开通。热线号码是_____。

8. 我用中文把酒店的名字写下来，您把它交给出租车司机。他会带您去那儿(车费大约是100元人民币)。

9. 您预定的是哪个酒店？

10. 这是英文版的北京/伦敦旅游指南。

11. 我不太确定。您最好去大厅问讯处问一下，他们会帮助您的。

12. You may claim your checked baggage in the Arrival Hall with your luggage tag.

13. You need to go through entry formalities in the Arrival Hall.

14. You may confirm your transit flight with ground staff.

15. You may go to the transit counter for your connecting flights.

16. Your next flight will take off in 4 hours. You've got plenty of time to make the transit.

12. 您可以凭行李牌在进港大厅领取您的托运行李。

13. 您需要去进港大厅办理入境手续。

14. 您可以与地面人员联系，确认您的转机航班。

15. 您可以去中转柜台办理转机手续。

16. 您的下一个航班在 4 小时后起飞，您的转机时间很充裕。

4.4.3　China Beijing(中国北京)

1. The Great Wall is regarded as a symbol of the ancient civilization of China.

2. The Palace Museum, also called the Forbidden City, was once the palace for emperors in Ming and Qing dynasties. It has a unique structural design.

3. The Tian'an Men Square is the largest city square in the world with an area of 440,000 square meters.

4. Beihai Park is an imperial garden with a history of over 800 years.

5. The Summer Palace is located on the northwest outskirts of Beijing, about 12 kilometers away from central Beijing. It is the best-preserved and largest imperial garden existing in the world. The Summer Palace was designated a World Heritage site by UNESCO in 1998.

6. Chinese traditional culture is profound, to name a few, Book of Changes, Qigong and Wushu, etc.

1. 长城被认为是中国古代文明的象征。

2. 故宫又名紫禁城，曾经是明清历代皇帝的宫殿，它的建筑风格非常独特。

3. 天安门广场是世界上最大的城市广场，面积44万平方米。

4. 北海公园是有 800 多年历史的皇家园林。

5. 颐和园位于北京市的西北郊，距市区约 12 公里，是世界上现存规模最大的皇家园林。1998年，颐和园被联合国教科文组织列入《世界遗产名录》。

6. 中国的传统文化博大精深，如易经、气功、武术。

7. Beijing National Stadium, the main competition venue of the 29th Olympic Games, is located in the south of Beijing Olympic Park.

8. The National Aquatics Centre is also known as "The Water Cube". The building's structural design is based on the natural formation of soap bubbles.

9. Chinese Wushu has a long history. It has gradually become an international event.

10. I recommend the Great Wall, which is a well-known tourist resort.

7. 北京国家体育场位于北京奥林匹克公园中心区南部，是第29届奥林匹克运动会的主体育场。

8. 国家游泳中心也称作"水立方"。它的结构设计是基于自然形成的肥皂泡。

9. 中国武术历史悠久，现在已成为世界性竞技项目。

10. 我建议您去参观长城，那是非常著名的景点。

4.4.4 Airport Service(机场服务)

1. Lavatory 63 in the rear doesn't function well. Would you please fix it?

2. How many portions of meal catered for this flight? Any special meals?

3. Can we change some cutleries for first and business class here? Any changes for the amount of meal carts or ovens?

4. Could you please speed up your cleaning? I'm afraid we'll be late.

5. Sir, we are ready for boarding.

6. Is there any special handling passenger on this flight? What's the reason for repatriation?

7. What did you do on the ground and how did you explain to PAX? We'd better give PAX the same explanations.

1. 后面63号卫生间有些故障，您能检修一下吗？

2. 请问这个航班备有多少份餐？有特殊餐吗？

3. 头等、公务舱的器皿可以更换吗？餐车、烤炉的数量有变更吗？

4. 麻烦您，打扫卫生的速度能稍快一点吗？恐怕我们要晚点了。

5. 先生，我们已经准备好登机了。

6. 请问这个航班上有特殊客人吗？遣返客人是什么原因？

7. 请问今天在飞机延误期间你们为旅客做了些什么？你们给旅客解释的原因是什么？最好我们给旅客的解释一致。

Words and Expressions

disembark [ˌdɪsɪmˈbɑːk] vt. & vi. 离船；下飞机

disembarkation [ˌdɪsˌembɑːˈkeɪʃn] n. 离船；下飞机

boarding bridge　登机桥

transit [ˈtrænzɪt] n. 运输；经过；中转

destination [ˌdestɪˈneɪʃn] n. 目的，目标；目的地

stroller [ˈstrəʊlə] n. 婴儿手推车

pram [præm] n. (手推的)婴儿车

boarding gate　登机口

shuttle bus　机场大巴；摆渡车；穿梭巴士

version [ˈvɜːʃn] n. 版本；译本

guidebook [ˈɡaɪdbʊk] n. 旅行指南

Information Counter　问讯处，服务台

assistance [əˈsɪstəns] n. 帮助，援助

tag [tæɡ] n. 标签

ancient [ˈeɪnʃənt] adj. 古代的；古老的

civilization [ˌsɪvəlaɪˈzeɪʃn] n. 文明

emperor [ˈempərə] n. 皇帝，君主

preserve [prɪˈzɜːv] vt. 保护；保持，保存；
　　　　　　n. 腌制食物

profound [prəˈfaʊnd] adj. 深厚的；意义深远的；严肃的；知识渊博的

stadium [ˈsteɪdiəm] n. 运动场；体育场

venue [ˈvenjuː] n. 会场；(事件或活动的)发生地，举办地点

Beijing National Stadium　北京国家体育场

Beijing Olympic Park　北京奥林匹克公园

aquatic [əˈkwætɪk] adj. 水生的，水栖的；水中的，水上的

National Aquatics Centre　国家游泳中心

Water Cube　水立方

structural [ˈstrʌktʃərəl] adj. 结构(上)的，构架(上)的

formation [fɔːˈmeɪʃn] n. 形成；构成，结构

Conversations on Board Part II

bubble [ˈbʌbl] *n.* 气泡；泡沫

resort [rɪˈzɔːt] *n.* 度假胜地

repatriation [ˌriːpætrɪˈeɪʃn] *n.* 遣送回国，归国

PAX *abbr.* = passengers 主要用于旅行社、饭店、航空公司等

4.5 Special Situations(特殊情况)

4.5.1 Explanation and Service(安抚)

1. For the flight safety, the ice on the aircraft has to be removed. Please wait for some more time and we will keep you informed once we have further information. Would you like something to drink?

2. We are waiting for some transit passengers. Please wait for some more time before we have further information.

3. The aircraft door has been closed. However, there is a lot of traffic right now, so we have to wait for the clearance from the air traffic control.

4. We are not allowed to take off now because of the bad weather in Dalian. We'll provide you with further information. If there is anything we can do for you, please let us know.

5. We have to wait for a few minutes due to a minor technical problem. Would you like something to drink?

6. We have to wait for _____ minutes due to the unfavorable weather conditions on our route. We'll provide you with further information.

7. We'll apply for the take-off clearance as soon as the weather is getting better.

1. 为了飞行安全，飞机需要除冰，请您再等一会儿，得到最新消息我们立即通知您。请问您需要喝杯饮料吗？

2. 我们正在等待部分转机旅客，得到最新消息我们会立即通知您。

3. 我们的飞机虽然关门了，但这时候起飞的飞机比较多，所以我们还需要等待塔台部门的指挥。

4. 大连的天气不好，我们的飞机不能起飞。我们会将有关信息及时广播通知您。如果您有什么需求，我们会尽力帮您解决。

5. 我们的飞机有些小故障，需要等待几分钟。您还需要喝些饮料吗？

6. 由于航路天气不好，我们还须等待_____分钟才能起飞。我们乘务组会随时将最新的信息告诉您。

7. 一旦天气转好，我们会尽快申请起飞。

8. We're now waiting for the take-off clearance, and there are 2 aircrafts lining up ahead of us. Please remain seated for the time being.

9. Thank you for your patience. We're now serving beverage and meal. Please tell us if there's anything else we can do for you.

8. 我们正在等待起飞的命令，现在飞机排在第三位。请您暂时留在座位上。

9. 感谢您的耐心等待。我们将为您提供饮料和餐食。如果有什么可以帮您，请告知我们。

4.5.2　Disembarkation(下客)

1. We have to change to another aircraft because of the mechanical trouble. Please disembark with all your belongings.

2. We'll inform the ground staff if you'd like to cancel the flight. They will help you do the relevant arrangement.

3. The flight has to be cancelled because Beijing Capital International Airport has been closed due to the bad weather.

4. As the waiting time is relatively long due to the bad weather in Shanghai, ground staff require PAX to disembark with belongings. They will provide you with further information.

1. 由于机械故障无法排除，我们需要换乘另一架飞机。请您下机时带好随身物品。

2. 如果您想取消今天的航班，我们会通知地面工作人员，帮助您办理相关手续。

3. 由于北京首都国际机场天气不好，机场已经关闭，为了大家的安全，机长决定取消今天的航班。

4. 由于上海机场天气暂时不能好转，我们还需要等待较长的时间，请您带好所有手提物品到候机室休息等候。地面工作人员会随时将最新消息广播通知您。

4.5.3　Complaint(投诉)

1. Certainly, we will do our best to help you. I will report this situation to my purser.

1. 好的，我们会想办法帮助您的。我先把这个情况报告给乘务长。

Conversations on Board Part II

2. Sir, I do apologize that *the South China Morning Post* is not available at this time. I will check it again in the cabin. Meanwhile, may I offer you an alternative newspaper or magazine?

3. Seat selling of our company is according to a certain standard.

4. Sorry, there is something wrong with the entertainment system in your seat. May I change a seat for you?

5. Please accept our apologies, madam. I understand you are feeling frustrated because you are trying to watch your movie. The chief purser is currently resetting the system so the PTV should restart soon. Thank you for your patience and understanding.

6. Madam, I am really very sorry and I understand your feeling. May I bring you a pair of earplugs?

7. May I bring you a pillow? It'll be more comfortable.

8. Thanks for your advice. We will keep on improving our service.

9. We greatly appreciate your comments(It is greatly appreciated if you make suggestions to our service).

10. Madam, I fully understand how upset and frustrated you are with your experience on this flight. I totally agree that this situation is inappropriate. I do sincerely apologize that we made you feel this way. Is there anything I can do to make the rest of your flight more enjoyable?

11. I am sorry our service does not meet your expectations. I will inform our manager about your feelings, and we will do our best to make the rest of your flight more enjoyable.

2. 先生，很抱歉《南华早邮》暂时没有了。过一会儿，我在客舱里再找找看是否还有。这其间，我给您拿些其他报纸或杂志好吗？

3. 我们公司的座位销售都是根据统一的标准实施的。

4. 对不起，您座椅的娱乐系统出故障了。我给您调换一下座位好吗？

5. 请接受我们的道歉，女士。我知道您很想看这部电影，所以我理解您的失望心情。主任乘务长正在重启系统，您的个人电视马上就恢复。谢谢您的耐心和理解。

6. 女士，对不起，我非常理解您现在的感受，我给您拿一副耳塞来好吗？

7. 我给您拿个枕头好吗？这样可以舒服一些。

8. 感谢您的建议，我们将继续改进我们的服务品质。

9. 非常感谢您对我们的服务提出宝贵意见。

10. 女士，我能理解您对这个航班感到不满，我完全同意这种状况是不对的。对此我诚心诚意地向您表示道歉。您看我还能做些什么能让您在接下来的旅途中感到满意？

11. 对不起，我们的服务没有达到您的期望。我会把您的意见向我们的经理汇报，我们也会尽全力让您在接下来的旅途中感到满意。

4.5.4　Lost & Found(失物认领)

1. Do you remember where you lost that luggage/item in the terminal? Would you please describe it?

2. May I have your name, telephone number and address? We will contact you when we find it. You may also call our Lost and Found Office at _____ for further information.

3. Sir/Madam, We are sorry that we've contacted the ground staff and they tried every means, but still could not find it.

1. 您在候机楼什么地方丢失的行李/物品？您能描述一下丢失的物品吗？

2. 您可否告诉我们您的姓名、电话、地址？我们找到后会及时与您取得联系。您还可以拨打这个失物认领处电话_____，询问您的物品。

3. 先生/女士，非常抱歉！我们已经联系了地勤工作人员，他们想尽了一切办法，但是仍然没有找到。

4.6　Special Passengers(特殊旅客)

4.6.1　UM(无人陪伴儿童)

1. May I help you put your small bag in the overhead compartment?

2. Here is the lavatory. Open the door like this. Once getting inside, switch this pin to latch. Do not hurt your hand while opening the door.

3. This is the call button in the lavatory.

4. Hi, boy/girl, do you have a pet name? May I call you _____?

5. Have you got two pieces of checked baggage?

1. 我可以帮你把你的小包放在行李架上吗？

2. 这是卫生间。这样开门。进去后通过这个销子插门。开门时小心别夹到你的手。

3. 这是卫生间内的呼叫铃。

4. 你好，男孩/女孩。你的小名叫什么？我可以叫你_____吗？

5. 你有两件托运行李吗？

6. I'll show you the way to your seat. Please let us know whenever you need help.

7. Hi, boy/girl. Here is the delicious child meal for you. Be careful! The entree is hot.

8. I'll keep your traveling documents and return ticket, and give them to the ground staff when you disembark.

6. 我会带你去座位。有什么事，随时告诉我们。

7. 你好，男孩/女孩。这是为你准备的儿童餐。小心！热食烫手。

8. 证件和回程机票先放在我这里保管，下机时我们会将这些证件一起交到地服人员的手中。

4.6.2 CIP(常旅客)

1. Mr./Ms. _____, thank you for your support to our company for such a long time.

2. I'm _____. I'm glad to be at your service. Here's the newspaper we prepared for you. If you need any assistance, please press the call button.

3. Sorry, it's our fault. Thank you for your support to our company for such a long time. What else can we do for you?

1. _____先生/女士，感谢您长期对我们航空公司的支持。

2. 我是_____今天很高兴能为您服务。这是我们为您准备的报纸。如果有什么需要，请按呼叫按钮。

3. 对不起！这是我们工作的疏忽。感谢您长期以来对我们公司的支持。我们还能为您做点什么？

4.6.3 Disabled Passengers(残疾旅客)

1. What is your seat number? May I assist you with your hand luggage?

2. May I show you the way to your seat? It is the window seat.

3. Would you mind holding my arm? I will take you to your seat if you like.

4. Would you like me to assist you to move into the seat?

1. 您的座位号是多少？我帮您拿行李好吗？

2. 请您跟我从这边走。靠窗的是您的座位。

3. 如果您愿意，您可以扶着我的胳膊，我带您走过去好吗？

4. 需要我协助您坐到座位上吗？

5. May I put your hand luggage under the seat for your convenience?

6. Relax (Take it easy). May I adjust the seat back and air vent for you? An air sickness bag is in the seat pocket in front of you. I'll be right back with a hot towel and water.

7. Your drink is in the paper cup. May I put it on the table?

8. Here is your meal. May I open it for you?

9. We are entering the cabin now. Please hang on to your chair.

10. The aisle in economy class is quite narrow. It will be safer to pull the wheelchair backward.

11. May I help you with your luggage when you disembark?

12. May I assist you to disembark when ground staff arrives with the wheelchair?

13. May I introduce the meal for you? Imagine the tray is like a dial plate. Salad is at the 12 o'clock and entree at 6. Please be aware that the entree is very hot.

14. I'm afraid the seeing-eye dog cannot take a passenger seat.

15. We've prepared an in-flight wheelchair for your convenience on board.

16. I am waiting outside. Please do not hesitate to call me if there is anything I can do for you.

17. May I put the crutches/walking cane/braces into the closet?

5. 我帮您把行李放在座椅下面吧，落地后提拿也会方便些。

6. 放松。我可以为您调一下座椅靠背和通风口吗？在您座椅前方口袋内有清洁袋，我去给您拿热毛巾和水，马上回来。

7. 饮料我帮您倒在纸杯里了，放在桌子上可以吗？(无臂残疾人只能用纸杯，塑料杯太硬无法用嘴咬住杯口。如果条件允许可为其提供吸管。)

8. 这是您的餐食。请问需要我帮您打开吗？

9. (提醒使用机上小轮椅的旅客) 我们现在进入客舱了，请您坐稳。

10. 普通舱的通道较窄，我们把轮椅倒着拉出来会安全一些。

11. 下机时我来帮助您拿行李好吗？

12. 地面工作人员和轮椅到达后，我来帮助您一起下机好吗？

13. (为视障乘客介绍餐食) 我帮您介绍一下餐食，好吗？餐盘的摆放如同时钟的表盘，在十二点位置是沙拉，六点的位置是热餐，小心别烫手！

14. (携带导盲犬的乘客) 对不起，恐怕导盲犬不能占用座位。

15. (轮椅乘客) 我们准备了机上轮椅，方便您在航程中使用。

16. (使用洗手间时) 我在外面等候您，如需要协助，请随时叫我。

17. 我帮您把拐杖/手杖/助步器放在衣帽间里吧？

4.6.4 Infants(婴儿)

1. The plane will be taking off soon. Let me help you fasten the infant seat belt!
2. For your baby's safety, I'll fix the basinet after take-off.
3. What a lovely girl/boy! For his/her safety, please be sure not to leave him/her unattended.
4. Sir/Madam, there is an infant seat belt. For the safety of your lovely baby, I will help you fasten it (let me help you fasten it).
5. You may use the changing board in the middle lavatory if your baby needs to get a change.
6. Here is the meal for you and your child. If you like one portion first, I may reserve the other one for you. You may call me whenever you want it.

---

1. 飞机马上就要起飞了，我帮您把婴儿安全带系好！
2. 为了孩子的安全，等飞机起飞后我会帮您把婴儿摇篮安置好。
3. 您的孩子真活泼，但为了他/她的安全，请不要让他/她离开您的视线。
4. 先生/女士，这是婴儿安全带。为了孩子的安全，我来帮您系好它。
5. 如果您需要给孩子更换尿布，请用中间的洗手间，那里有专用更换板。
6. 这是您和孩子的餐食。您看是一起用，还是我帮您先留存一份？需要时，我们随时为您提供。

4.6.5 Sickness(不适或疾病)

1. Judged by the symptoms, it might be air-sickness.
2. Please don't worry. I will make an announcement to see if there are any medical personnel on board.
3. We can make some arrangement if you need an airport ambulance. Some charge will be necessary for their service.
4. Please don't worry. It's caused by the change of air pressure.
5. The discomfort can be relieved by swallowing saliva or chewing candy. You will get better when the plane comes to the cruising level.

---

1. 从症状分析，您可能是晕机。
2. 别着急，我将广播为您找大夫。
3. 如果您需要，我们可以帮助您联系机场救护车。他们会收取一定费用。
4. 请别担心。这是由于气压的改变引起的。
5. 您可以通过吞咽口水或吃点糖果来减轻疼痛，等飞机平飞后您就会好一点儿。

6. It is helpful to pinch your nose and blow air into your inner ears or to open your mouth wide.

7. Madam, please don't worry about flying. The captain is very experienced and Air China has excellent flying records. May I offer you some chrysanthemum tea? I also suggest that you listen to some soothing music, as this will help you relax.

6. 如果您捏住鼻子鼓鼓气或者张张嘴，会管用的。

7. 女士，请不必担心飞行。我们的机长非常有经验，中国国际航空公司保持着极好的飞行纪录。我给您送一杯菊花茶好吗？我建议您听些轻音乐，因为这能帮助你放松。

4.7　Emergency Situation(紧急情况)

1. Let me demonstrate how to use the oxygen mask.
2. Brace for impact according to my instructions.
3. Don't panic! Follow our directions!
4. Bend over and hold your ankles.
5. Don't put anything in the seat pocket in front of you.
6. Release seat belt. Come this way.

1. 我来为您示范一下氧气面罩的使用方法。
2. 请您根据我的口令和动作做好防冲击姿势。
3. 不要惊慌！请听从我们的指挥！
4. 弯下身，抓住脚踝。
5. 请不要把任何东西放在您前面的座椅口袋里。
6. 解开安全带，到这边来！

Words and Expressions

standard [ˈstændəd] *n.* 标准，规格
frustrated [frʌˈstreɪtɪd] *adj.* 挫败的，失意的，泄气的
inappropriate [ˌɪnəˈprəʊpriət] *adj.* 不恰当的，不适宜的
sincerely [sɪnˈsɪəli] *adv.* 真诚地；诚恳地
entree [ˈɒntreɪ] *n.* 主菜
UM　无人陪伴儿童
CIP　常旅客

Conversations on Board Part II

disabled [dɪsˈeɪbld] *adj.* 残废的，有缺陷的

wheelchair [ˈwiːltʃeə] *n.* 轮椅

crutch [krʌtʃ] *n.* 拐杖；支撑

walking cane　　[医]步行手杖

infant [ˈɪnfənt] *n.* 婴儿，幼儿

airsickness [ˈeəsˈɪknəs] *n.* 晕机

ambulance [ˈæmbjələns] *n.* 救护车

discomfort [dɪsˈkʌmfət] *n.* 不舒适，不舒服；不安

pinch [pɪntʃ] *vt.* 捏，掐；挤痛

impact [ˈɪmpækt] *n.* 影响；作用；冲击力

release [rɪˈliːs] *vt.* 释放；放开；发布；发行

oxygen mask　　(供人吸氧时用的)氧气面罩

bend [bend] *vt.* (使)弯曲，屈身；拉弯

ankle [ˈæŋkl] *n.* 踝，踝关节；脚脖子

Practice

Ⅰ. Look and Say

Guess the meaning of the given pictures, both in English and in Chinese.

　　　1　　　　　　　　　　　2　　　　　　　　　　　3

4

5

6

7

8

9

Conversations on Board Part II

10

11

12

14

13

15

16

17

18

Conversations on Board Part II

II. Word Matching

Match the words in Column A with their definitions in Column B.

1

Column A

belongings
overhead
compartment
arrange
fragile
upgrade
procedure
regular
cooperation
process

Column B

(1) orderly, even, or symmetrical(规则的：有秩序的、均匀的或对称的)

(2) a series of actions, changes, or functions bringing about a result(过程，程序：一系列导致某一结果的行动、变化或作用)

(3) located, functioning, or originating from above(上面的，高架的：位于上部的，在上方运转的或来源于上部的)

(4) to raise to a higher grade or standard(把……提高到一个更高的水平或标准)

(5) to put into a specific order or relation; dispose(安排：进行有序或相关的排列；布置)

(6) a manner of proceeding; a way of performing or effecting something(程序，进程，影响：方式；进行或完成某事的途径)

(7) the act or practice of cooperating(合作的行为或实践)

(8) one of the parts or spaces into which an area is subdivided(隔间；舱：把一块面积分割的几个部分或几个空间之一)

(9) easily broken, damaged, or destroyed; frail(脆的：易被打碎的、易被破坏或毁坏的；脆弱的)

(10) personal items that one owns; possessions(个人所有物；拥有物)

2

Column A

- compliance
- regulation
- forbid
- location
- airbus
- turbulence
- lavatory
- reserve
- alternative
- terminate

Column B

(1) a principle, rule, or law designed to control or govern conduct(规章制度：为控制或管理行为而设计的原则制度或法律)

(2) to command (someone) not to do something(不许：命令某人不能干某事)

(3) the act of complying with a wish, request, or demand; acquiescence(顺从：顺从别人希望、要求、命令的行为；默认)

(4) allowing or necessitating a choice between two or more things(二选一的：允许或必须对两个或更多的事物作选择的)

(5) a commercial passenger jet with a short to medium range(空中巴士：小型至中型的各种商业客运机)

(6) to keep back, as for future use or for a special purpose (保留，收藏：保留，如用于将来使用或某一特殊的目的)

(7) a room equipped with washing and often toilet facilities; a bathroom(厕所：通常装有清洗和厕所设施的房间；盥洗室)

(8) an eddying motion of the atmosphere that interrupts the flow of wind(湍流：打断风的运动的极不规则的大气运动)

(9) a place where something is or could be located; a site(地点：某物所在或可在的地方；地点)

(10) to bring to an end or a halt(使终止：使其停止或停顿)

3

Column A

preserve
aquatic
profound
disembark
martial
transit
resort
destination
formation
version

Column B

(1) conveyance of people or goods from one place to another, especially on a local public transportation system (运输：把人或货物从一个地方运到另一个地方，尤指通过本地公共运输系统的运送)

(2) the place to which one is going or directed (目的地：一个人要到达的地方)

(3) to leave a vehicle or aircraft(下车，下飞机：离开车辆或飞机)

(4) to maintain in safety from injury, peril, or harm; protect(保护：使免于损害，危险或伤害而处于安全中)

(5) of, relating to, or suggestive of war(战争的：战争的，与战争有关的，暗示战争的)

(6) consisting of, relating to, or being in water(水生的，水栖的：由水构成，与水有关或在水中的)

(7) the act or process of forming something or of taking form(形式，组成：给予某种东西形状或使之获得形状的动作或过程)

(8) a place frequented by people for relaxation or recreation (常去的地方，胜地：人们为放松和消遣常去的地方)

(9) thoroughgoing; far-reaching(深远的：贯穿整个的；意义深远的)

(10) an adaptation of a work of art or literature into another medium or style(版本：一件文学或艺术作品向另一种媒介或形式的改编)

4

Column A

bend
impact
sincere
appropriate
crutch
infant
release
frustrate
standard
ambulance

Column B

(1) an acknowledged measure of comparison for quantitative or qualitative value; a criterion(标准：一种公认的衡量数量或者质量的标准；标准)

(2) to cause feelings of discouragement or bafflement in(丧气：引起受挫或泄气的情绪)

(3) suitable for a particular person, condition, occasion, or place; fitting(适合于……的：适合于某特定的人，条件，事件或地点的；适宜的)

(4) being without hypocrisy or pretense; true(真诚的：不虚伪的或不假装的；诚实的)

(5) a staff or support used by the physically injured or disabled as an aid in walking, usually designed to fit under the armpit and often used in pairs (拐杖：身体受伤或致残者用来辅助其走路用的支架，长度通常到达腋窝，常成对使用)

(6) a child in the earliest period of life, especially before he or she can walk(婴儿，幼儿：处于生命早期阶段的小孩，尤指他或她还不会走路之时)

(7) a specially equipped vehicle used to transport the sick or injured(救护车：有特殊装备的车辆，用来运送病人或伤员)

(8) the striking of one body against another; collision(碰击，撞击：一个物体对另一个物体的击打；碰撞)

(9) to set free from confinement, restraint, or bondage(赦免：从限制、约束或束缚中释放出来)

(10) to cause to assume a curved or angular shape(使弯曲：使变弯曲或使成角度)

III. Dialogue Completion

In the following dialogues, some sentences have been removed. Choose the most suitable one from the list to fit into each of the numbered blank, and then work in pairs and act as the flight attendant and the customer according to the dialogue.

1. There is a card in your seat pocket that shows you where your nearest exit is.
2. I would be happy to help you clarify anything you need help with.
3. The most important thing you can do is keep your seat belt fastened when the captain asks you to.
4. Your oxygen mask is above you, next to the reading light.

A: Can I ask you some questions about the in-flight instructions?
B: _____
A: Could you help me find out where my nearest exit is?
B: _____ Yours is two rows in front of you.
A: Where is my oxygen mask that you were talking about?
B: _____ It will drop down when you need it.
A: I am concerned about landing in the water.
B: The life jackets are under your seat. You can also use your seat cushion as a flotation device.
A: What is the most important thing we can do to stay safe?
B: _____

IV. Cloze Test

In this part, the words are missing in the following paragraph. Choose the most appropriate words from the following form.

| take-off | oxygen | on | demonstration | ensure |
| duty | maximum | evacuation | release | safety |

After boarding, an important __(1)__ in taking care of the passengers is to brief them on the use of their __(2)__ belts, and on any relevant emergency procedures. The safety __(3)__ at the beginning of a flight is very important. For example, aircraft seat belts, like the seats, consist of a lap-strap and sometimes a shoulder harness. The passengers must be shown how to fasten, adjust and __(4)__ their seat belts. Cabin crew must always check that they are fastened at __(5)__ and landing. The passengers should be shown how to put __(6)__ a life jacket, and how to use the emergency __(7)__ masks stored above the seat. Aircraft cabins can become stuffy, so __(8)__ that there is adequate ventilation and each passenger knows, how to adjust the appropriate vent to __(9)__ personal comfort. Handicapped passengers may need special attention, and a modified briefing to explain how they should leave the airplane in the case of an __(10)__. Passengers need not be passive.

Ⅴ. Translation and Practice

1. Translate the following sentences into English.

A：打扰一下，先生您要点什么，中餐还是西餐？

_____

B：我要中餐。

_____

A：请放下身前的桌子，那样比较舒适。

_____

B：噢，谢谢。服务真周到。

_____

A：乐意效劳。您要喝点什么呢，牛奶、茶、咖啡、橙汁，还是冰水？

_____

B：我要一杯豆奶，有吗？

_____

A：好的，给您。用餐愉快。

_____

B：非常感谢。噢，打扰一下，我可以要双份吗？我还想要点辣椒酱。

_____

A：好的，请慢用，先生。

_____

B：噢，给你添麻烦了。我想问一下这是什么肉。

_____

A：是的，这是牛肉。您爱吃吗？

_____

B：还可以。非常感谢。

_____

Conversations on Board Part II

A：不客气。如果需要任何服务请按那个按钮。

2. Check your answer and practice with your partner in your group.

A：Excuse me, sir. What would you like to eat, Chinese food or western food?

B：I'd like to have Chinese food.

A：Please put down the table in front of you. It's more comfortable that way.

B：Oh, thank you. So nice you are.

A：It's my pleasure. What would you like to drink, milk, tea, coffee, orange juice or iced water?

B：I want a cup of bean milk. Do you have any?

A：Yes, here you are. Enjoy your meal.

B：Thanks a lot. Oh, excuse me. Can I have it in double? And I want some chili paste.

A：OK, enjoy yourself, sir.

B：Oh, sorry to bother you. I want to know what kind of meat it is.

A：It is beef. Do you like it?

B：That's OK. Thanks very much.

A：You are welcome. Please press that button if you need any help.

3. In this part, there are ten sentences in English. Each of the sentences is followed by four choices of suggested translation marked A, B, C, and D. Make the best choice and write the corresponding letter.

(1) Cabin attendants make face-to-face contact with passengers. (   )

　　A. 空中乘务员与乘客进行面对面的谈话。

　　B. 空中乘务员与乘客进行面对面的交往。

　　C. 客舱乘务员与乘客进行紧密的互动。

　　D. 客舱乘务员与乘客进行脸对脸的联系。

(2) You may find the safety instruction card and some magazines in the seat pocket. (   )

　　A. 你可以在椅背的袋子中找到安全指引卡和一些杂志。

　　B. 你可以在椅背的袋子中找到安全须知卡和一些报纸。

　　C. 在椅背的袋子中你可以找到安全须知手册和杂志。

　　D. 在椅背的袋子中你可以找到安全须知手册和报纸。

(3) If the passenger has any checked baggage, it is dealt with at the check-in desk. (   )

　　A. 如果旅客有行李托运，在登记签到处办理。

B. 如果旅客有行李托运，在值机柜台办理。

C. 如果旅客有需过安检的行李，在值机柜台办理。

D. 如果旅客有需检查的行李，在登记签到处办理。

(4) International airports must have customs areas, currency exchange counters and so on. (   )

A. 国际机场必须有旅客休息区、货币兑换柜台等。

B. 国内机场必须有旅客休息区、现金兑换柜台等。

C. 国际机场必须有海关区、货币兑换柜台等。

D. 国内机场必须有海关区、现金兑换柜台等。

(5) Cabin attendants must perform their own assigned duties. (   )

A. 乘务员必须清楚自身应尽的职责。

B. 乘务员必须遵守乘务员相关规定。

C. 乘务员必须缴纳指定的税款。

D. 乘务员必须履行指定的职责。

(6) Please walk in this direction. Don't leave things in the aisle. (   )

A. 请沿着这条直线走，过道里不能留东西。

B. 请按照这个方向走，过道里不能留东西。

C. 请按照这个方向走，不要把东西堆放在过道里。

D. 请沿着这条直线走，不要把东西堆放在过道里。

(7) Moslem meals apply to a large number of passengers from the Middle East. (   )

A. 印度餐供应给很多中东乘客。

B. 印度餐适合很多中部和东部的乘客。

C. 穆斯林餐适合很多中东乘客。

D. 穆斯林餐供应给很多中部和东部的乘客。

(8) Liquor and tobacco sales have continued to grow in volume. (   )

A. 酒和烟草的销售量一直在增长。

B. 酒和烟草的销售量一直在减少。

C. 珠宝和烟草的销售量一直未减少。

D. 珠宝和烟草的销售量一直未增长。

(9) The boarding music is played until five minutes before take-off but not during the flight. (   )

A. 登机音乐要等到飞机起飞前 5 分钟才会播放，但在航班飞行期间不播放。

B. 登机音乐要等到飞机起飞后 5 分钟才会播放，但在航班飞行期间一直播放。

C. 登机音乐一直播放到飞机起飞前 5 分钟，但在航班飞行期间不播放。

D. 登机音乐一直播放到飞机起飞后 5 分钟，但在航班飞行期间不播放。

(10) All exits are equipped with exit signs above and adjacent to the exits. (　　)

A. 出口的上方和附近都配备有出口标志。

B. 出口的上方都标有出口标志，并指向出口。

C. 出口上都标有出口标志，出口标志就在出口附近。

D. 出口的上方都配备有指向出口的出口标志。

(11) They must provide a courteous and efficient service to the passengers. (　　)

A. 他们必须为乘客提供礼貌而高效的服务。

B. 他们必须为乘客提供热情而高效的服务。

C. 他们必须为乘客提供热情而真诚的服务。

D. 他们必须为乘客提供礼貌而真诚的服务。

(12) Please refrain from smoking. (　　)

A. 请远离烟雾。

B. 请继续吸烟。

C. 请不要吸烟。

D. 请不要靠近吸烟区。

(13) Your life vests are stowed under your seats, and the magazines are in the seatback pockets. (　　)

A. 氧气面罩储存在座位下方，杂志在椅背的袋子中。

B. 救生衣储存在座位底下，杂志在椅背的袋子中。

C. 救生衣储存在座位底下，报纸在后方椅子的口袋中。

D. 氧气面罩储存在座位下方，报纸在后方椅子的口袋中。

(14) Your carry-on luggage must not exceed the regulated weight. (　　)

A. 托运行李不得超过规定重量。

B. 托运行李不得低于规定重量。

C. 随身携带行李不得低于规定重量。

D. 随身携带行李不得超过规定重量。

(15) Lunch and dinner consist of basically the same dishes. (　　)

A. 中餐、晚餐菜式的道数是一样的。

B. 中餐、晚餐食品构成基本相同。

C. 中餐、晚餐食品构成完全相同。

D. 中餐、晚餐食品构成几乎都不相同。

(16) Adjust the volume button to the proper place you like. (　　)

　　A. 请按动音量按钮，调节你所喜欢的音量。

　　B. 请将音量按钮移放到你喜欢的位置。

　　C. 请调节容量按钮，调节到你认为合适的容量。

　　D. 请将音量按钮放置在你喜欢的位置。

(17) Cabin attendants must show the passengers how to fasten, adjust and release their seat belts. (　　)

　　A. 客舱乘务员必须向乘客示范怎样系、调整和松开皮带。

　　B. 乘客必须向客舱乘务员展示系、调整和松开皮带的方法。

　　C. 乘客必须向客舱乘务员展示系、调整和松开安全带的方法。

　　D. 客舱乘务员必须向乘客示范怎样系、调整和松开安全带。

(18) As we all know, there is emergency and survival equipment on board all aircraft. (　　)

　　A. 当我们都知道时，飞机上装有紧急和救生设备。

　　B. 当我们都知道时，飞机甲板上装有应急和救生设备。

　　C. 正如我们所知，飞机甲板上有应急和导航设备。

　　D. 正如我们所知，飞机上有紧急和救生设备。

(19) Modern airports provide such facilities as runways, apron, and passenger terminal areas, etc. (　　)

　　A. 现代化机场有跑道、滑行道和旅客终端区域等设施。

　　B. 现代化机场提供像跑道、停机坪、候机楼这样的设施。

　　C. 新式机场提供像跑道、停机坪和旅客终端区域这样的设施。

　　D. 新式机场提供跑道、滑行道和候机楼等设施。

Ⅵ. Reading Comprehension

In this part, there are 2 passages. Each of them is followed by 5 questions. To each question, there are four possible answers marked with A, B, C, and D. Please choose the correct or best answer to each question.

Passage 1

Cabin attendants need to see that passenger seat belts are fastened tightly and that no smoking rule is observed. Then they will report the result of this check to the purser. Special care must be taken in checking the seat belts of certain types of passengers, especially the elderly, handicapped passengers, unaccompanied minors and others.

When there are infants among the passengers, cabin attendants should ensure that infants are seated so that there are sufficient oxygen masks for all the passengers in the row. For small children, it is recommended that a blanket be placed behind them so that the seat belt can hold them more securely.

Other checks must be made, such as confirming that all compartments, carts and containers are locked and they are secured by stoppers where these are fitted, confirming that window shades are open for take-off, all trays are stowed and the seatbacks are in the upright position.

(1) Before taking off, cabin attendants do the safety check and inform _____ of the result. ( )

 A. the captain   B. the purser

 C. the controller   D. the flight engineer

(2) When checking the seat belts of passengers, cabin attendants should take special care of _____. ( )

 A. the elderly   B. handicapped passengers

 C. unaccompanied minors   D. all of the above

(3) Which of the following statement is NOT true? ( )

 A. Cabin attendants can give small children a blanket to place behind them.

 B. Passengers must fasten their seat belts tightly when taking off.

 C. When in an emergency, the infants cannot have enough oxygen masks.

 D. Unaccompanied minors are permitted to travel by air alone.

(4) Other "checks" should be made before take-off EXCEPT _____. ( )

 A. confirming that all compartments are locked

 B. confirming that all carts and containers are empty

 C. confirming that window shades are open

 D. confirming that all trays are stowed

(5) For take-off, passengers' seatbacks should be _____. ( )

 A. in the upright position   B. inclined forward

 C. very clean   D. kept balance

Passage 2

The Boeing 747-400 airplane has reached its cruising altitude of 10km and cruising(巡航) speed of 900km per hour on its way from London to Beijing. The purser has announced that the passengers are now free to unfasten their seat belts and move around the cabin, however, passengers should keep their seat belts fastened when seated.

The passenger cabin layout consists of three sections. The 747-400 is unique in having two decks. On the upper deck, behind the flight crew there is the first class section. On the lower deck, at the front is the business class section for passengers who pay the full fare, while at the back is the much larger economy section for passengers who have special cheap rate tickets.

The stewards and stewardesses — 14 in all — are now busy around the galleys. A choice of drinks, followed by dinner, video entertainment including a film and finally breakfast in the morning is the order of service. Individual headphones are distributed, and these, when plugged into the arm of the seat — give a variety of in-flight musical programs. Also in the arm of the seat are the controls for a personal reading light, fresh air control and call button.

Dinner is served on special prepared trays, perhaps prawn cocktail, followed by a choice of roast chicken or braised steak with chocolate mousse to finish. The chicken and beef has been heated in the special microwave ovens in the galleys. It is hard to believe that a hot, three-course meal can be served while the plane is flying at this altitude and speed.

Dinner over, the cabin lights are dimmed, the blinds by the windows are drawn, the screens unfold and the film begins. Now, for the first time the cabin crew take it in turns to have a rest while the passengers watch the film or snooze dreaming of arriving in Beijing in the morning.

(1) When the plane is flying, the passengers _____ when seated. (   )

    A. are free to talk

    B. are free to come into the flight deck

    C. are advised to fasten their seat belts

    D. must unfasten the seat belts

(2) The passenger cabin layout consists of the following three sections EXCEPT _____. (   )

    A. the first class   B. the cockpit

    C. the business class   D. the economy class

(3) During the flight, the cabin attendants should do the following EXCEPT _____. (   )

    A. collect the passengers' passports

Conversations on Board Part II

   B. serve the drinks

   C. serve the meals

   D. give out headsets

(4) Before the meal, the cabin attendants should heat _____ in the ovens in the galley. (   )

   A. the chocolate mousse

   B. the salad

   C. the chicken and beef

   D. the snacks

(5) During the film, the cabin attendants will _____. (   )

   A. wake up the passengers so they don't miss the film

   B. watch the film with the passengers

   C. have a chat in the cabin

   D. have a rest in turn

VII. Situational Practice

Form pairs to discuss the following questions. Make up short conversations based on the following roles and settings. Representatives will be asked to put forward their answers in the front.

1. A passenger is smoking in the cabin before take-off. How do you stop him?

2. A passenger wants to read a copy of local newspaper.

3. One of the passengers is thirsty and asks for something to drink, and you list several kinds of drinks on board for him to choose.

4. A passenger with a baby doesn't know how to fasten her seat belt. What would you say to help her?

5. A passenger wants to read a copy of *Financial Times*.

6. A young lady asks for dessert after main course, and you introduce dessert to her.

7. A passenger puts her baggage near the emergency exit before take-off. Stop her and explain to her.

8. You are serving a couple. The wife asks for a cup of plain coffee while the husband asks for some beer which has run out. You advise them to have some tea instead.

9. A passenger forgets to fasten her seat belt before take-off. Please remind her.

Ⅷ. Further Study

1. 凤凰知音(Phoenix Miles)

2013年，中国国际航空股份有限公司宣布将原有常旅客计划"国航知音"正式更名为"凤凰知音"。国航及国航系成员公司深圳航空、澳门航空、山东航空、北京航空、大连航空及西藏航空将实现在同一常旅客计划平台上运营。

"凤凰知音"是国航面对航空市场普遍疲软现象做出的主要对策之一，通过将各航空公司的资源统一整合，使国航系各航空公司共享资源，如原来不是星空联盟的澳门航空、山东航空也可以享受星空联盟所属成员公司的航空里程累积及其服务等。由于系统已经搭建完成，因此凡持有国航系航空公司会员卡的乘客可以直接享受"凤凰知音"的服务。

国航系整合资源之后，"凤凰知音"会员数量达到2,500万人。"凤凰知音"常旅客计划是一项遍及世界的里程奖励活动，拥有35家航空公司合作伙伴，以及200多家非航空合作伙伴。"凤凰知音"会员在签约合作伙伴处消费，均可参加累积里程换取奖励机票、奖励升舱等活动。其服务资源遍及北京、上海、成都、广州及港澳台等主要城市和地区，覆盖餐饮娱乐、旅游休闲、银行理财、时尚和运动健康等多个领域。

2. 航空管制

航空管制亦称飞行管制，是有关部门根据国家颁布的飞行规则，对空中飞行的航空器实施的监督控制和强制性管理的统称。其主要目的是维持飞行秩序，防止航空器互撞和航空器与地面障碍物相撞。

我国民用航空对领空的使用范围有明确规定，超过民用航空范围的空域由我国国防部队——中国人民解放军空军单位进行管理。乘坐飞机旅行时，经常可能遇到空中交通管制而变更航线、目的地、起落时间。有序的空中管制是保证所有旅客和空域安全的必要程序。一般理解的航空管制是前面所说的狭义航空管制。实际上，一切的航空行为，包括航空附属的地面设施、资源的管理、使用调度都是在依照航空管制的内容进行，航空管制可以说是所有民航行为的基本原则，是一个广义的规则。

3. 无人陪伴儿童

"无人陪伴儿童"(Unaccompanied Minors，UM) 服务，是指乘坐飞机时为无成人(年满18周岁且有民事行为能力的人)同行的年满5周岁未满12周岁的儿童，办理的儿童无陪护手续服务。也就是通常所说的"儿童托运"。如果孩子年满12周岁但未满18周岁，也可自愿申请无成人陪伴儿童服务。目前中国不承办联程航班的无成人陪伴儿童业务。

在国际及地区航线上，为孩子申请无成人陪伴儿童服务，须交纳无成人陪伴服务费。单程直达运输费用为人民币 260 元或等值货币。有些航空公司对办理无成人陪伴儿童手续在时间上有限制，如有些航空公司限在航班起飞前一个星期提出申请，有些航空公司限在航班起飞前三天提出申请。

为单独乘机旅行的儿童申请无成人陪伴服务时，须提供申请者的身份证件以及儿童的有效护照等旅行证件。同时应准确提供送机人及接领人的姓名、住址、联系电话，以便和送机人及接领人保持联络。

孩子乘机时须持有效旅行证件、《无成人陪伴儿童运输申请书》，以及客票、收费单等，并将文件和证件一并装入文件袋内，挂于儿童的胸前，办理交接手续。

在飞机起飞及抵达目的地机场时，航空公司有专人协助儿童办理乘机登记、海关、安检和提取行李等手续，并在候机期间专人负责照管儿童及其文件袋；并会亲手将儿童交给乘务长，让儿童安全顺利地完成空中之旅。

抵达接机时，航空公司会根据儿童的乘机信息事先与接领人取得联系。当航班落地后，承运人会安排专人迎接儿童，并与乘务员办理交接手续，协助儿童办理到达手续。接领人在到达站须出示有效身份证件，地面服务人员经核对无误后会将儿童交给接领人。

4. 常旅客计划

常旅客(Commercially Important Person，CIP)，即重要客户旅客，是一种身份的象征，一般比 VIP 的等级低，而又比普通旅客的等级高。

常旅客计划(Frequent Flyer Program)是指航空公司、酒店等行业向经常使用其产品的客户推出的以里程累积或积分累计奖励里程为主的促销手段，是吸引公商务旅客、提高公司竞争力的一种市场手段。常旅客计划实际上也被称为客户忠诚计划(Loyalty Program)。早在 20 世纪 80 年代初，航空公司就开始引入常旅客计划，取得了一定的效果。随后世界上几乎所有的航空公司都有了自己的常旅客计划。因而航空公司的常旅客计划被认为是民航史上最成功的市场创新活动。

(1) 国内常旅客计划。

目前中国国内的常旅客计划有以下几种。

国航常旅客奖励计划：凤凰知音。

东航常旅客奖励计划：东方万里行。

南航常旅客奖励计划：明珠俱乐部。

海航常旅客奖励计划：金鹏俱乐部。

昆航常旅客奖励计划：尊享俱乐部。

川航常旅客奖励计划：金熊猫计划。

厦航常旅客奖励计划：白鹭卡。

春航常旅客奖励计划：绿翼会员积分计划。

(2) 国际常旅客计划。

国际常旅客计划有以下3种。

① 天合联盟常旅客计划。

如果加入了天合联盟会员航空公司的常旅客计划，则可以通过该账户在天合联盟的所有承运商中赢取和兑换里程数，并享受天合联盟的各项优惠。

该联盟旗下的航空公司常旅客计划具体如下。

俄罗斯国际航空公司：Aeroflot Bonus。

阿根廷航空公司：Aerolineas Plus。

墨西哥航空公司：Club Premier。

西班牙欧洲航空公司：Flying Blue 蓝天飞行。

法航荷航集团：Flying Blue 蓝天飞行。

意大利航空公司：MilleMiglia。

台湾中华航空公司：华夏里程酬宾计划。

中国东方航空公司：东方万里行。

中国南方航空公司 明珠俱乐部。

捷克航空公司：OK Plus。

达美航空：Sky Miles 飞凡里程常客计划（与西北航空合并）。

肯尼亚航空公司：Flying Blue 蓝天飞行。

大韩航空公司：SkyPass。

罗马尼亚航空公司：Flying Blue 蓝天飞行。

越南国家航空公司：金莲卡。

厦门航空公司：白鹭卡。

② 星空联盟常旅客计划。

无论是哪家星空联盟成员航空公司常旅客计划的会员，都可以通过搭乘星空联盟各成员航空公司的航班累积里程、兑换奖励，同时取得相应身份级别。

该联盟旗下的航空公司常旅客计划具体如下。

中国国际航空公司：Phoenix Miles 凤凰知音。

深圳航空公司：Phoenix Miles 凤凰知音。

加拿大航空公司：Aeroplan。

汉莎航空公司：Miles & More。

亚德里亚航空公司：Miles & More。

奥地利航空公司：Miles & More。

布鲁塞尔航空公司：Miles & More。

波兰航空公司：Miles & More。

克罗地亚航空公司：Miles & More。

瑞士国际航空公司：Miles & More。

韩亚航空公司：Asiana Club。

新加坡航空公司：KrisFlyer。

塔姆航空：Fidelidade。

土耳其航空：Miles & Smiles。

爱琴海航空公司：Miles and Bonus。

新西兰航空公司：Airpoints。

美国联合航空公司：MileagePlus 前程万里(与美国大陆航空合并)。

巴拿马航空公司：MileagePlus 前程万里。

埃塞俄比亚航空公司：ShebaMiles。

埃及航空公司：Egyptair Plus。

北欧航空公司：EuroBonus。

南非航空公司：Voyager。

葡萄牙航空公司：Victoria。

阿维安卡塔卡航空公司：LifeMiles。

泰国航空公司：Royal Orchid Plus。

全美航空公司：Divident Miles。

③ 寰宇一家常旅客计划。

每个寰宇一家(oneworld)成员航空公司都独立提供各自的飞行常旅客奖励计划。当其会员乘坐其联盟中的航班时，都可以获得相应的里程/积分，以及会员会籍级别，并在兑换里程时，可在"寰宇一家"遍及全球的 800 多个目的地中任意选择。

该联盟旗下的航空公司常旅客计划具体如下。

柏林航空公司：Topbonus。

美国航空公司：AAdvantage。

英国航空公司：Executive Club。

国泰航空公司：MarcoPolo 马可波罗会(包括港龙航空公司)。

芬兰航空公司：Finnair Plus。

西班牙航空公司：Iberia Plus。

日本航空公司：JAL Mileage Bank。

智利航空公司：Lan Pass。

澳大利亚航空：Frequent Flyer。

皇家约旦航空：Royal Plus。

西伯利亚航空：S7 Priority。

Part III

Announcements

Unit 5　　Domestic Cabin Announcements

(国内机舱广播)

5.1　Prior to Take-off(起飞前)

5.1.1　Welcome(欢迎词)

Ladies and gentlemen,

Welcome aboard Air China, a proud Star Alliance member. This flight is CA_____ to _____.

We feel grateful to all passengers and Phoenix Miles members for your business, and you are very much welcome to join the Phoenix Miles, our frequent flyer program.

As we are preparing for take-off, please fasten your seat belt, switch off your mobile phone and any kind of electronic devices.

Highly appreciated for your patience and understanding during the waiting time.

Here we have for you a video explaining the safety features of the aircraft.

All of our staff members hope you will enjoy the flight and wish you a pleasant journey.

Thank you!

女士们，先生们：

欢迎您选乘星空联盟成员中国国际航空公司 CA_____航班前往_____。

非常感谢各位旅客、国航知音会员长期以来对国航的支持与信赖，真诚邀请更多旅客加入国航常旅客计划。

我们就要准备起飞了，请您系好安全带并关闭手机等电子设备。

对于您在等待时所表现出的耐心与理解，我们深表感谢！

先为您播放安全须知录像，请留意收看。

我们全体机组成员将竭诚为您服务。祝您旅途愉快。

谢谢！

5.1.2 Safety Demonstration(安全演示)

Ladies and gentlemen,

We will now explain the use of the life vests, oxygen masks and seat belts, and show you the location of the emergency exits.

Your life vest is located under your seat. To put the vest on, slip it over your head.

Fasten the buckles and pull the straps tightly around your waist.

To inflate the vest, pull down firmly on the tabs, but do not inflate in the cabin.

If your vest needs further inflation, you can pull the mouth-pieces from either side of the upper part of the vest and blow into the tubes.

Your oxygen mask is located in a compartment above your head. It will drop automatically in case of emergency.

Pull the mask firmly toward yourself to start the flow of oxygen.

Place the mask over your nose and mouth and slip the plastic band over your head. In a few seconds, the oxygen will begin to flow.

Your seat belt contains two pieces. To fasten the belt, slip one piece into the buckle and pull the belt tightly.

Please keep your seat belt fastened securely when you are seated.

There are _____ emergency exits on this aircraft. They are located in the front, the rear, the middle, and the upper deck.

女士们，先生们：

现在客舱乘务员向您介绍救生衣、氧气面罩、安全带的使用方法和应急出口的位置。

救生衣位于您座椅下面的口袋里。使用时取出，经头部穿好。

将带子围在腰上扣好、系紧。

然后打开充气阀门。但客舱内不要充气。

充气不足时，请将救生衣上部的两个人工充气管拉出，用嘴向里充气。

氧气面罩储藏在您头顶的上方，发生紧急情况时面罩会自动脱落。

氧气面罩脱落后，请用力向下拉面罩。

将面罩罩在口鼻处，把袋子套在头上。几秒钟后，便可进行正常呼吸。

在座椅上有两条可以对扣起来的安全带，将带子插进带扣，然后拉紧。

当您就座时，请系好安全带。

本架飞机共有_____个应急出口，分别位于前部、后部、中部和上舱。

In the event of an evacuation, emergency floor-lights will illuminate a darkened cabin, leading you to these exits.

The safety instruction is in the seat pocket in front of you. Please read it carefully as soon as possible.

Thank you!

在应急撤离时，紧急照明指示灯将照亮黑暗的地方，引导您到应急出口。

在您前方座椅口袋里有安全说明书，请您尽早阅读。

谢谢！

5.1.3　Seat Belt Confirmation Prior to Take-off (起飞前确认系好安全带)

Ladies and gentlemen,

Our plane will be taking off shortly. Please confirm that your seat belt is securely fastened and your electronic devices are completely switched off.

Thank you!

女士们，先生们：

我们的飞机马上就要起飞了。请您再次确认系好您的安全带，并关闭手机等电子设备。

谢谢！

5.1.4　Domestic Order of Service(国内航线及服务介绍)

Ladies and gentlemen,

It is Mid-autumn Festival. Wish you a happy Mid-autumn.

Our plane has left _____ for _____. The distance between _____ and _____ is _____ kilometers and the flight time is _____ hour(s) and _____ minutes. We are expected to arrive at our destination at about _____ A.M./P.M.

女士们，先生们：

今天是中秋节，在此祝您中秋快乐！

我们的飞机已经离开_____前往_____，由_____到_____的飞行距离是_____公里，预计空中飞行时间是_____小时_____分。我们大约将在上午/下午_____抵达目的地。

Announcements Part III

Code Sharing Flight

This is code sharing flight with _____ (name of airline).

Please keep your seat belt fastened when you are in your seat in case we encounter any unexpected turbulence. Smoking is prohibited throughout the flight. All mobile phones must be switched off during the flight.

We will soon be serving _____ (breakfast/lunch/dinner/snacks/refreshment/brunch). A complete selection of beverages will accompany the service.

Enjoy our in-flight programs. Select the audio channel that corresponds to the program you will be watching. If you need any assistance, please let us know.

We hope you will enjoy the flight. Thank you!

代号共享

本次航班是国航和_____航空公司的代号共享航班。

当您在座位上休息时，请系好安全带以防我们遇到突发的气流颠簸。我们的航班全程禁止吸烟。为了保证飞行安全，请您全程关闭手机，包括带有飞行模式的手机。

我们即将为您提供 _____（早餐/午餐/晚餐/小吃/茶点/早中餐）。我们还为您准备了各种酒水饮料。

我们将要为您放映娱乐节目，请您根据观看的节目选择相应的声音频道。如果您需要帮助，请与乘务员联系。

再次祝您旅途愉快！
谢谢！

Words and Expressions

aboard [əˈbɔːd] *prep.* 在(船、飞机、火车)上，上(船、飞机、火车)
  adv. 在船(飞机、火车)上，上船(飞机、火车)
alliance [əˈlaɪəns] *n.* (国家、政党等的)结盟，同盟，联盟
automatically [ˌɔːtəˈmætɪklɪ] *adv.* 自动地；无意识地
buckle [ˈbʌkl] *vt. & vi.* 用搭扣扣紧；(使)变形，弯曲
  n. 带扣，扣环
confirm [kənˈfɜːm] *vt.* 确认；证实
electronic [ɪlekˈtrɒnɪk] *adj.* 电子的；用电子操纵的

emergency [ɪˈmɜ:dʒnsɪ] *n.* 紧急情况；突发事件

evacuation [ɪˌvækjʊˈeɪʃən] *n.* 撤空；撤离

frequent [ˈfri:kwənt] *adj.* 频繁的，经常发生的

inflate [ɪnˈfleɪt] *vt. & vi.* 使充气(于轮胎、气球等)；(使)膨胀；(使)涨价

illuminate [ɪˈlju:mɪneɪt] *vt.* 照亮，照明；阐明，说明

location [ləʊˈkeɪʃən] *n.* 位置，场所；定位；外景(拍摄地)

mask [mæsk] *n.* 面具；假面具；用作掩饰的事物；面膜

oxygen [ˈɒksɪdʒən] *n.* 氧，氧气

phoenix [ˈfi:nɪks] *n.* 凤凰

prior [ˈpaɪə] *adj.* 优先的；占先的；事先安排的

securely [sɪˈkjʊrlɪ] *adv.* 安全地；牢固地

strap [stræp] *v.* 用带捆扎；包扎(伤口)
　　　　　　　　n. 带子

switch off　关掉，关上

vest [vest] *n.* 马甲；背心；(印有运动员编号的)运动背心

5.2　Prior to Landing(着陆前)

5.2.1　Before Landing(着陆前)

20/30 Minutes Prior to Landing	着陆前 20/30 分钟
Ladies and gentlemen,　　We will be arriving at _____ airport in 20/30 minutes. The temperature is _____ degrees Centigrade or _____ degrees Fahrenheit.　　As the outside temperature is relatively high/low, we suggest you take off/put on your coat when you disembark.	女士们，先生们：　　本次航班大约在 20/30 分钟后到达_____机场。_____的地面温度为_____摄氏度，_____华氏度。　　由于机舱外温度相对较高/低，建议您适当减少/增加衣物。

Announcements

As we prepare for landing, please return your seatback to the upright position, secure your table and footrest, open the window shades and make sure that your seat belt is securely fastened. All electronic devices must be switched off at this time. You must not turn on your mobile phone until the cabin doors are open.

(Night flight) We are about to dim the cabin light. If you would like to read, we suggest you use your reading light.

Thank you!

飞机已经开始下降,请调直座椅靠背、收起小桌板及脚踏板、打开遮光板并系好安全带。为了避免干扰驾驶舱内的飞行仪器,请关闭所有电子设备,在舱门开启前请您不要打开手机。

(夜航)稍后我们将调暗客舱灯光,需阅读的旅客,建议您打开阅读灯。

谢谢!

5.2.2 Farewell and Giving Regards(着陆前致意)

Ladies and gentlemen,
On behalf of the entire crew, we would like to thank you for your support and cooperation during the flight.
Thank you!

女士们,先生们:
对您在旅途中给予的支持和帮助,我们全体机组成员表示最诚挚的谢意。
谢谢!

5.2.3 Video Demonstration of the Transit Procedures (中转流程的视频演示)

Ladies and gentlemen,
All transit passengers, may I have your attention, please? We have for you a video explaining the transit procedures. We hope it helps.
Thank you!

女士们,先生们:
所有需要转机的旅客请注意,现在将为您播放一段转机流程解说视频,希望它能帮到您。
谢谢!

5.2.4 Announcement of Transit Flights(中转航班通告)

Ladies and gentlemen,

All transit passengers, may I have your attention please? This is the announcement about transit flights.

Passengers for _____ on CA_____, please proceed to the boarding gate _____;

Passengers transferring to other Air China flights with baggage that has been checked to the final destination, please proceed to the transit counter directly.

If your final destination is Beijing, You may claim your checked baggage at baggage carousel No. _____.

Thank you!

女士们，先生们：

所有需要转机的旅客请注意，下面将为您播放一则中转航班信息。

前往_____的旅客，您乘坐的CA_____航班，登机口在_____号。

转乘国航其他国内或国际航班，且已办理行李联运的旅客，请下机后直接前往中转服务柜台办理转乘手续。

北京为终点的旅客，托运行李请在_____号传送带提取。

谢谢！

5.2.5 Seat Belt Confirmation Before Landing (落地前确认系好安全带)

Ladies and gentlemen,

Our plane will be landing shortly. Please confirm that your seat belt is securely fastened.

Thank you!

女士们，先生们：

我们的飞机马上就要着陆了。请您再次确认系好您的安全带。

谢谢！

5.2.6 Transit(中途着陆)

Ladies and gentlemen,

We have just landed at _____ airport _____ terminal. The temperature is _____ degrees Centigrade or _____ degrees Fahrenheit outside the cabin.

女士们，先生们：

我们已经到达_____机场，您将在_____号候机楼进港。机舱外的温度为_____摄氏度，_____华氏度。

Our plane is taxiing, so please remain seated with your seat belt fastened and luggage stowed. The use of mobile phone is prohibited until the seat belt sign is switched off. And we remind you to use caution when opening the overhead compartments. Passengers continuing on to _____, please disembark with your belongings, head to the waiting hall and wait there for the boarding call.

Highly appreciated for your patience and understanding during the waiting time.

Thank you for flying Air China, a member of the Star Alliance network. We hope you'll enjoy your stay in _____.

Good-bye!

飞机还将滑行一段距离，在安全带指示灯熄灭以前，请您系好安全带，在座位上耐心等候。在此期间，请不要打开手机。下机时请小心开启行李箱，以免行李滑落。继续前往_____的旅客，请带好全部手提物品到候机室休息，等候广播通知上飞机。

对于您在等待时所表现出的耐心与理解，我们深表感谢！

感谢您选乘星空联盟成员中国国际航空公司航班。祝您在_____愉快！

再见！

5.2.7　Terminal Landing(终点着陆)

Ladies and gentlemen,

We have just landed at _____ airport (Welcome to _____ airport). Please remain seated with your seat belt fastened and luggage stowed. The use of mobile phone is prohibited until the seat belt sign is switched. And we remind you to use caution when opening the overhead compartments.

The temperature is _____ degrees Centigrade, _____ or degrees Fahrenheit.

Please take all your belongings with you when you disembark.

女士们，先生们：

我们已经到达_____机场(欢迎您到达_____机场)，飞机还将滑行一段距离，在安全带指示灯熄灭以前，请您系好安全带，在座位上耐心等候。在此期间，请不要打开手机。下机时请小心开启行李箱，以免行李滑落。

机舱外的温度为_____摄氏度，_____华氏度。

下机请携带好您的随身物品。

Passengers holding Air China boarding pass for connecting flights, please go through the immigration formalities. In compliance with Chinese customs regulations, you are subject to customs inspection with all your belongings.

We will remove any unidentified baggage from the aircraft for security reason.

Highly appreciated for your patience and understanding during the waiting time.

Thank you for flying Air China, a member of the Star Alliance network. We hope you'll enjoy your stay in _____.

Good-bye!

继续转乘国际航班的旅客，请您在本站办理出境手续。根据中华人民共和国海关规定，请将您的手提行李带下飞机，接受海关检查。

对遗留在飞机上的、未经海关检查的行李物品，将由地面服务人员交海关处理。

对于您在等待时所表现出的耐心与理解，我们深表感谢！

感谢您选乘星空联盟成员中国国际航空公司航班，我们期待与您下次旅途再会，祝您在_____愉快！

再见！

Words and Expressions

carousel [ˌkærəˈsɛl] *n.* (机场的)行李传送带

centigrade [ˈsentɪɡreɪd] *n.* 摄氏温度

destination [ˌdestɪˈneɪʃən] *n.* 目的地，终点

dim [dɪm] *adj.* 暗淡的，昏暗的
    vt. & vi. (使)变暗淡；(使)变模糊；(使)减弱

Fahrenheit [ˈfærənˌhaɪt] *n.* 华氏温度(冰点为 32 度，沸点为 212 度)

footrest [ˈfʊtˌrɛst] *n.* 脚凳

shortly [ˈʃɔrtlɪ] *adv.* 立刻，马上

waiting hall 候机大厅

transfer [trænsˈfɜː] *vt. & vi.* (使)转乘，(使)换乘，(使)改乘

upright [ˈʌpˌraɪt] *adj.* 直立的；垂直的；正直的；诚实的

Announcements Part III

Practice

I. Look and Say

Tell the names of the items on board according to the given pictures, both in English and in Chinese.

1

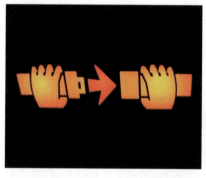
2

3

4

5

6

7

8

9

10

Ⅱ. Word Matching

Match the words in Column A with their definitions in Column B.

Column A

secure
phoenix
switch
evacuation
illuminate
prior
inflate
confirm
alliance
automatic

Column B

(1) a close association of nations or other groups, formed to advance common interests or cause(联盟，同盟；结盟：国家或其他集团为了促进其共同利益或事业而组成的紧密联盟)

(2) mythological birds of East Asia that reign over all other birds. Traditionally people think its appearance means the appearance of good times. In China and Japan it was a symbol of the imperial house, and it represented "fire, the sun, justice, obedience, and fidelity"(东亚地区神话传说中的百鸟之王。传统观念认为，它的出现则意味着盛世的出现。在中国和日本它曾是皇室的象征，它代表着"火，太阳，正义，服从和忠诚")

(3) to fill something with air or gas so as to make it swell(充气：使空气或其他气体充入某物使之膨胀)

(4) acting or operating in a manner essentially independent of external influence or control(自动的：以一种基本上不受外界影响或控制的方式行动或操作的)

(5) the act of evacuating or the condition of being evacuated(撤离：撤离的行为或被撤离的状态)

(6) to provide or brighten with light (照明，照亮：给予光亮或用光使发亮)

(7) preceding in time or order(在前的，在先的：在时间或次序上居先的)

(8) to support or establish the certainty or validity of; verify(证实：支持或确认……的肯定性或有效性；确认)

(9) free from danger or attack(安全的：没有危险或免受攻击的)

(10) a small control for an electrical device which you use to turn the device on or off(用于电气装置的开关控制)

III. Announcement Completion

Fill in the blanks with words or expressions given, and then work in pairs to read aloud to each other.

Announcement 1

| take-off | switch off | appreciated | welcome | grateful |
| frequent | features | flyer | flight | aircraft |

Ladies and gentlemen,

  Welcome aboard Air China, a proud Star Alliance member.

  This flight is CA1689 Beijing to Harbin.

  We feel ___(1)___ to all passengers and Phoenix Miles members for your business, and you are very much ___(2)___ to join the Phoenix Miles, our ___(3)___ ___(4)___ program.

  As we are preparing for ___(5)___, please fasten your seat belt, ___(6)___ your mobile phone and any kind of electronic devices.

  Highly ___(7)___ for your patience and understanding during the waiting time.

  Here we have for you a video expanding the safety ___(8)___ of the ___(9)___.

  We hope you will enjoy the ___(10)___ and wish you a pleasant journey.

  Thank you!

Announcement 2

| seat belts | vest | straps | buckles | put |
| slip | pull | inflate | blow | fasten |

Ladies and gentlemen,

  We will now explain the use of the life vests, oxygen masks and ___(1)___, and show you the location of the emergency exits.

  Your life ___(2)___ is located under your seat. To ___(3)___ the vest on, ___(4)___ it over your head.

  Fasten the ___(5)___ and ___(6)___ the ___(7)___ tightly around your waist.

  To ___(8)___ the vest, pull down firmly on the tabs, but do not inflate in the cabin.

  If your vest needs further inflation, you can pull the mouth-pieces from either side of the upper part of the vest and ___(9)___ into the tubes.

Your oxygen mask is located in a compartment above your head. It will drop automatically in case of emergency.

Pull the mask firmly toward yourself to start the flow of oxygen.

Place the mask over your nose and mouth and slip the plastic band over your head. In a few seconds, the oxygen will begin to flow.

Your seatbelt contains two pieces. To ___(10)___ the belt, slip one piece into the buckle and pull the belt tightly.

Announcement 3

| stowed | prohibited | caution | compartments | disembark |
| regulations | security | inspection | switched | compliance |

Ladies and gentlemen,

We have just landed at Beijing Capital International Airport, terminal 1. Please remain seated with your seat belt fastened and luggage ___(1)___.

The use of mobile phone is ___(2)___ until the seat belt sign is ___(3)___. And we remind you to use ___(4)___ when opening the overhead ___(5)___.

The temperature is 30 degrees Centigrade or 86 degrees Fahrenheit.

Please take all your belongings with you when you ___(6)___.

(Arrival in Beijing)

Passengers holding Air China boarding pass for connecting flights, please go through the immigration formalities. In ___(7)___ with Chinese customs ___(8)___, you are subject to customs ___(9)___ with all your belongings.

We will remove any unidentified baggage from the aircraft for ___(10)___ reason.

Highly appreciated for your patience and understanding during the waiting time.

Thank you for flying Air China, a member of the Star Alliance network. We hope you'll enjoy your stay in Beijing.

Good-bye!

Ⅳ. Further Study

1. 应急出口

应急出口就是飞机上设置的"飞机安全门"。客机上除了登机门、厨房服务门等正常开启的门以外,还有平时不开,专为紧急情况发生后才开启的应急出口。

应急出口是客机应急救生设施的一种。坐在飞机紧急出口的旅客承担着"应急员"责任。紧急出口舱门非常重,旅客要有足够力气才能打开它。如果旅客认为自己无力操作,那么就要将座位让给有能力的人。因此,坐在这个位置的旅客,在享受宽敞座位的同时,也要承担起"守护者"的责任。既然是紧急出口,上面的开门机构就不可以随意触动。在打开紧急门时,一定要按照乘务员的指导或紧急门上的操作说明来进行,以便其能及时打开。通常在没有机组人员的通知下,旅客不得自行打开紧急门。

一般来说,航空公司地服会锁住紧急出口的一排座位号,不在网上、自助登机机器上公开发放。依据规定,不能把紧急出口座位发放给老人、不足15岁儿童、孕妇、行动不便和照顾婴儿的旅客,以及缺乏良好中文语言表达能力、听觉和视觉能力、信息传达能力的旅客。

通常情况下,一些年轻力壮、有多次飞行经验的旅客会乘坐这类座位。在飞行和降落过程中,如果发生意外事故,在机长发出指令疏散乘客时,坐在紧急出口的人,应该协助空乘人员打开紧急出口舱门,放置好逃生滑梯或气垫,协助其他乘客逃生。

值机柜台工作人员在为旅客办理应急出口座位时,会向旅客说明出口座位的相关规定和注意事项,并用明确的语言询问旅客是否愿意履行紧急出口座位旅客职责,同时为旅客发放"紧急出口提示卡"。在未得到旅客承诺以前,工作人员不得将旅客安排在紧急出口位置。

经常乘坐飞机的旅客一般都会留意座位后口袋里的一张《紧急出口座位须知》。这张座位须知详细说明了乘客应该具有什么能力和如何履行相关职责。

在起飞前,虽然空乘人员会告知"禁止拉动紧急出口的手柄"等,但是坐在紧急出口的旅客还是有必要了解一下紧急出口舱门的打开分解图,自己先弄明白怎样打开紧急出口。

另外,坐在紧急出口附近的旅客不能将自己的行李放在紧急出口处。

2. List of major festivals

Major Chinese Festivals		
Date	Chinese Name	English Name
农历一月一日	春节	The Spring Festival
农历一月十五日	元宵节	The Lantern Festival
4月5日	清明节	Tomb-sweeping Day
农历五月初五	端午节	the Dragon Boat Festival
农历八月十五	中秋节	the Mid-autumn Festival
9月10日	教师节	Teachers' Day
农历九月九日	重阳节	Double-ninth Day
10月1日	国庆节	National Day
农历十二月三十日	除夕	Chinese New Year's Eve

续表

Major Western and International Festivals		
Date	Chinese Name	English Name
1月1日	新年	New Year
2月14日	情人节	Valentine's Day
二月中、下旬	狂欢节	Carnival
3月8日	国际妇女节	Women's Day
3月15日	世界消费者权益日	World Consumer Right Day
4月1日	愚人节	April Fool's Day
春分月圆之后第一个星期日	复活节	Easter
5月1日	国际劳动节	Labor Day
6月1日	国际儿童节	Children's Day
11月第四个星期四	感恩节	Thanksgiving Day
12月24日	平安夜	Christmas Eve
12月25日	圣诞节	Christmas Day
12月26日	节礼日	Boxing Day
12月31日	新年除夕	New Year's Eve

3. List of meals

snacks(小吃)：crackers(薄脆饼干)、peanuts(花生)

refreshment(快餐)：sandwiches(三明治)、biscuits(饼干)、hamburgers(汉堡)

breakfast(早餐)

brunch(早午餐)

lunch(午餐)

dinner(晚餐)

tray snacks(盘点)、box snacks(盒点)

late night supper(夜宵)

Unit 6　International Cabin Announcements

(国际机舱广播)

6.1　Prior to Take-off(起飞前)

6.1.1　Welcome(欢迎词)

Ladies and gentlemen,

Welcome aboard Air China a proud Star Alliance member. This flight is CA＿＿＿＿ to ＿＿＿＿.

We feel grateful to all passengers and Phoenix Miles members for your business, and you are very much welcome to join the Phoenix Miles, our frequent flyer program.

As we are preparing for take-off, please fasten your seat belt, switch off your mobile phone and any kind of electronic devices.

Highly appreciated for your patience and understanding during the waiting time.

Here we have for you a video expanding the safety features of the aircraft.

We hope you will enjoy the flight and wish you a pleasant journey.

Thank you!

女士们，先生们：

欢迎您选乘星空联盟成员中国国际航空公司 CA＿＿＿＿航班前往＿＿＿＿。

非常感谢各位旅客、国航知音会员长期以来对国航的支持与信赖，真诚邀请更多旅客加入国航常旅客计划。

我们就要准备起飞了，请您系好安全带并关闭手机等电子设备。

对于您在等待时所表现出的耐心与理解，我们深表感谢！

先为您播放安全须知录像，请留意收看。

我们全体机组成员将竭诚为您服务。祝您旅途愉快。

谢谢！

6.1.2 Safety Demonstration(安全演示)

Ladies and gentlemen,

We will now explain the use of the life vests, oxygen masks and seat belts, and show you the location of the emergency exits.

Your life vest is located under your seat. To put the vest on, slip it over your head.

Fasten the buckles and pull the straps tightly around your waist.

To inflate the vest, pull down firmly on the tabs, but do not inflate in the cabin.

If your vest needs further inflation, you can pull the mouth-pieces from either side of the upper part of the vest and blow into the tubes.

Your oxygen mask is located in a compartment above your head. It will drop automatically in case of emergency.

Pull the mask firmly toward yourself to start the flow of oxygen.

Place the mask over your nose and mouth and slip the plastic band over your head. In a few seconds, the oxygen will begin to flow.

Your seat belt contains two pieces. To fasten the belt, slip one piece into the buckle and pull the belt tightly.

Please keep your seat belt fastened securely when you are seated.

女士们,先生们:

现在客舱乘务员向您介绍救生衣、氧气面罩、安全带的使用方法和应急出口的位置。

救生衣在您座椅下面的口袋里,使用时取出,经头部穿好。

将带子围在腰上扣好、系紧。

然后打开充气阀门。但客舱内不要充气。

充气不足时,请将救生衣上部的两个人工充气管拉出,用嘴向里充气。

氧气面罩储藏在您头顶的上方,发生紧急情况时面罩会自动脱落。

氧气面罩脱落后,请用力向下拉面罩。

将面罩罩在口鼻处,把袋子套在头上。几秒钟后,便可进行正常呼吸。

在座椅上有两条可以对扣起来的安全带,将带子插进带扣,然后拉紧。

当您就座时,请系好安全带。

There are _____ emergency exits on this aircraft. They are located in the front, the rear, the middle, and the upper deck.

In the event of an evacuation, emergency floorlights will illuminate a darkened cabin, leading you to these exits.

The safety instruction is in the seat pocket in front of you, please read it carefully as soon as possible.

Thank you!

本架飞机共有_____个应急出口，分别位于前部、后部、中部和上舱。

在应急撤离时，紧急照明指示灯将照亮黑暗的地方，引导您到应急出口。

在您前方座椅口袋里有安全说明书，请您尽早阅读。

谢谢！

6.1.3　Seat Belt Confirmation Prior to Take-off (起飞前确认系好安全带)

Ladies and gentlemen,

Our plane will be taking off shortly. Please confirm that your seat belt is securely fastened and your electronic devices are completely switched off.

Thank you!

女士们，先生们：

我们的飞机马上就要起飞了。请您再次确认系好您的安全带，并关闭手机等电子设备。

谢谢！

Announcements Part III

6.1.4 International Order of Service(国际航线及服务介绍)

Ladies and gentlemen,

Today is Christmas. Wish you a Merry Christmas.

Our plane has left _____ for _____. The distance between _____ and _____ is _____ kilometers and the flight time is _____ hour(s) and _____ minutes. There is a one hour time difference between _____ and _____. We are expected to arrive at our destination at about local time _____ A.M./P.M.

Code Sharing Flight

This is code sharing flight with _____ (name of airline).

Please keep your seat belt fastened when you are in your seat in case we encounter any unexpected turbulence. Smoking is prohibited throughout the flight. All mobile phones must be switched off during the flight.

We will soon be serving _____ (breakfast/lunch/dinner/snacks/refreshment/brunch/). A complete selection of beverages will accompany the service.

Enjoy our in-flight programs. Select the audio channel that corresponds to the program you will be watching. If you need any assistance, please let us know.

We hope you will enjoy the flight.

Thank you!

女士们，先生们：

今天是圣诞节，在此祝您圣诞快乐！

我们的飞机已经离开_____前往_____，由_____到_____的飞行距离是_____公里，预计空中飞行时间是_____小时_____分。_____和_____之间有一小时的时差。我们预计在当地时间(上午/下午)_____到达。

代号共享

本次航班是和_____航空公司的代号共享航班。

当您在座位上休息时，请系好安全带以防遇到气流颠簸。我们的航班全程禁止吸烟。为了保证飞行安全，请您全程关闭手机，包括带有飞行模式的手机。

我们即将为您提供_____(早餐/午餐/晚餐/小吃/快餐/早中餐)。我们还为您准备了多种冷热饮料。

本次航班为您准备了娱乐节目，敬请您欣赏。您可根据您观看的节目选择相应的声音频道。如果您需要帮助，请与乘务员联系。

再次祝您旅途愉快！

谢谢！

6.1.5　Quarantine (General)[检疫规定(通用)]

Ladies and gentlemen,

Quarantine regulations of _____ (country/region) do not allow fresh fruit, flowers, meat products, dairy products or any other plant or animal products to be brought into _____ (country/region).

If any of those has been brought into the flight, then we suggest you dispose of it before arrival.

We have for you a video "_____ (country/region) Quarantine for Air Travelers". We hope it helps.

Thank you!

女士们，先生们：

根据_____(国家/地区)的检疫规定，旅客不能携带水果、鲜花、肉类、奶类或其他动、植物制品入境_____(国家/地区)。

如果这些已被带上飞机，那么建议您在落地前将其处理掉。

我们将为您播放一段_____(国家/地区)航空旅客检疫录像片，希望对您有所帮助。

谢谢！

6.1.6　Quarantine in Italy(意大利检疫规定)

Ladies and gentlemen,

Italian quarantine regulations do not allow dried fish, dried shrimps, kelps, longans, herbs and other items of animal or plant origin to be brought into the country.

If any of those has been brought into the flight, then we strongly suggest you dispose of it before arrival.

We have for you a video "Italy Quarantine for Air Travelers". We hope it helps.

Thank you!

女士们，先生们：

根据意大利的规定，旅客不能携带干鱼、干虾、海带、桂圆、中草药品等各种动、植物制品和食品入境。

如果这些已被您带上飞机，那么我们强烈建议您在落地前将其处理掉。

我们将为您播放一段意大利旅客检疫录像片，希望对您有所帮助。

谢谢！

6.1.7 Quarantine in Australia(澳大利亚检疫规定)

Ladies and gentlemen,

Subject to Australian quarantine regulations, please declare the origin of all food items such as meat, cheese, fruit and other items of animal or plant on your Incoming Passenger Card.

Alternatively, place these items in the bins in the arrival concourse. All food you have taken with you must be left on board. Remember, your baggage will be X-rayed or screened on arrival.

Please fill in your Incoming Passenger Card carefully, as false declarations result in fines or prosecution on the spot.

We will play you a video on "Australian Quarantine for Air Travelers". Please watch carefully.

Thank you!

女士们，先生们：

根据澳大利亚的检疫规定，请在您的旅客入境卡中申报所有食品如肉类、奶酪、水果或其他动、植物制品的来源。

或者，请将这些物品放在到达地的收集箱内。所有的机上供应食品必须留在飞机上，到达后您的行李将接受 X 射线检查。

请认真填写您的入境卡，因为申报错误会导致您被当场罚款甚至起诉。

我们将为您播放一段澳大利亚检疫录像片，请您注意收看。

谢谢！

6.1.8 Quarantine in Japan(日本检疫规定)

Ladies and gentlemen,

In compliance with Japanese quarantine regulations, soil, plants with soil, pests, rice straw, paddy, fresh fruit and vegetables are not allowed to be brought into the country.

If any of those has been brought into the flight, then we suggest you dispose of it before arrival.

We have for you a video "Japanese Quarantine for Air Travelers". We hope it helps.

Thank you!

女士们，先生们：

根据日本的检疫规定，旅客不能携带土壤、带土壤的植物、病虫、稻草、稻谷、新鲜水果和蔬菜入境。

如果这些已被您带上飞机，那么请您在落地前将其处理掉。

我们将为您播放一段日本的检疫录像片，希望对您有所帮助。

谢谢！

6.1.9 Entry Documents and Immigration Regulations (入境及海关规定)

Ladies and gentlemen,

For your convenience to go through the formalities of entry, we'll play a video "entry guide". Please watch carefully.

After the video, we will distribute immigration and customs forms. Both forms need to be completed prior to arrival and submitted to customs and immigrations.

All Chinese citizens including mainland citizens, Hong Kong, Macao and Taiwan residents and overseas Chinese need not to complete entry forms. But all passengers may need to declare the flight number and show the agents the ticket or boarding pass when going through the immigration.

Thank you.

Good-bye!

女士们，先生们：

为了方便您办理入境手续，我们将播放一段"入境指南"录像节目，请您注意收看。

在视频播放完之后，我们将为您发放入境卡和申报单。这两种单据您需在落地前填好，落地后交给移民局和海关检查站。

所有中国公民(包括内地居民、港、澳、台居民及华侨)入境回国免填入境登记卡。但所有旅客在办理入境手续时，需主动说明所乘航班号，并请保留机票或登机牌，以便核准。

谢谢。

再见！

6.1.10 Completion of Landing Forms(美国申报单填写)

Ladies and gentlemen,

We will now distribute immigration and customs forms. The United States government requires that the landing form be completed by all passengers before arrival. U.S. passport holders, immigrants, Green Card holders or Canadian citizens do not need to complete the landing forms.

Passengers who are entering the United States under the Non-Immigrant Visa Waiver Programs should complete the form which is also available. Besides, all passengers are required to complete U.S. customs declaration forms. Only one form is necessary for a family traveling together.

女士们，先生们：

我们即将为您提供入境卡及海关申报单。美国政府规定，持有美国签证入境的旅客，必须填写这两种表格。美国公民、移民和绿卡持有人以及加拿大公民，只需填写海关申报单。

以非移民签证豁免计划进入美国的旅客应填写该表格。此外，所有乘客都需要填写美国海关申报单。每个家庭只填写一份海关申报单。

Announcements

We will now play a video explaining how to fill in the forms necessary for entry into the United States.

This is Air China flight _____. We are expected to arrive at our destination on _____ (day of the week) _____ (month) _____ (day). If you have any difficulty in completing the forms, please let us know.

Thank you!

现在我们为您播放一段录像，介绍如何填写这些表格，这些表格对您入境美国很重要。

本班航班号是_____，到达日期是_____月_____日，星期_____。如有疑问，请向乘务员查询。

谢谢！

6.1.11 Japanese Immigration Regulations(日本入境规定)

Ladies and gentlemen,

According to Japanese immigration regulations, immigration agents will collect the finger-print and facade photo of all non-Japanese citizens on the spot.

For your convenience, we'll play a video to help you complete the immigration form.

Thank you!

女士们，先生们：

根据日本的入境规定，所有非日本国籍旅客在到达日本机场后，要进行指纹和正面照片的采集。

为了您的方便，我们将播放一段视频，帮助您填写入境单。

谢谢！

6.1.12 German Immigration Regulations(德国入境规定)

Ladies and gentlemen,

According to the regulations of German immigration, all incoming passengers should sign your passport.

For your convenience, we'll play a video to help you complete the immigration form.

Thank you!

女士们，先生们：

根据德国移民局的规定，所有入境旅客需在护照内旅客签名一栏中，签上本人姓名。

为了您的方便，我们将播放一段视频，帮助您填写入境单。

谢谢！

Words and Expressions

agent [ˈeɪdʒənt] *n.* 代理人；代理商；特工

citizen [ˈsɪtɪzən] *n.* 公民；国民；市民

distribute [dɪˈstrɪbjut] *vt.* 分配，散布；分布

for your convenience　为了方便起见

Green Card　绿卡

holder [ˈhəʊldə] *n.* 支持物；持有者；持有人

immigrant [ˈɪmɪɡrənt] *n.* 移民

immigration [ˌɪmɪˈɡreɪʃən] *n.* 移居入境；移民人数；移民局检查处

incoming [ˈɪnˌkʌmɪŋ] *adj.* 进来的；正到达的

Macao [məˈkaʊ] *n.* 澳门

mainland [ˈmenˌlænd] *n.* 大陆；本土

　　　　　　adj. 大陆的；本土的

Non-Immigrant Visa Waiver Programs 非移民签证豁免计划

overseas [ˌəʊvəˈsiːz] *adv.* 在海外；在国外；向国外

　　　　　　adj. 来自海外的，外国来的

program [ˈprəʊˌɡræm] *n.* 程序；节目，节目单

submit to　向……呈交，递送……；顺从，屈从，服从……

visa [ˈviːzə] *n.* 签证

waiver [ˈweɪvə] *n.* 弃权声明书

6.2　During Flight(飞行期间)

6.2.1　Cruising(平稳航行中)

> Ladies and gentlemen,
> We will be dimming the cabin lights to allow you to relax and rest better during the flight.

> 女士们，先生们：
> 为了给您营造一个良好的休息环境，我们将调暗客舱灯光。

Announcements — Part III

If you would like to read, an individual reading light is available at your seat. If you wish to use a blanket, please fasten your seat belt over it.

We suggest that passengers sitting next to the window lower the window shades to keep out the sunlight.

If there is anything we can do for you, please let us know.

We wish you a pleasant flight.

Thank you!

如果您需要阅读，请打开您座位上方的阅读灯。如果需要使用毛毯，请将安全带扣在毛毯外。

我们建议坐在靠窗位置的旅客请拉下遮光窗帘。

在整个航程中，我们愿意随时为您提供服务。

祝您旅途愉快。

谢谢！

6.2.2 Duty-free Sales(出售免税品广播)

Ladies and gentlemen,

Duty-free merchandises are coming.

Please be advised that duty-free items bought at airports or on board may be carried in a sealed bag accompanied by a receipt of purchase. The bag should be kept sealed from the point of purchase until arrival at your destination.

You can also book other duty-free items in the booking card in case they are not available on this flight. We will try our best to get them at the next flight you specify.

Thank you!

女士们，先生们：

我们现在出售免税品。

请将在机场或飞机上购买的免税物品保持封口，将收据放在袋内，并保留收据以备查验。该购物袋从购买处到目的地要一直保持封口状态。

如果您在本次航班中未选择到满意的商品，您可以通过填写免税品预订单预订所需商品，我们会在您指定的下一段航班上尽力满足您的需要。

谢谢！

6.2.3　Health Video(健康养生视频)

Ladies and gentlemen,
We'll arrive at _____ airport in _____ hours. A video containing health and fitness tips will be played to make your flight more comfortable. _____(lunch/dinner/breakfast/snack/refreshment) will be served ten minutes after the video.
Thank you!

女士们，先生们：
我们的飞机将在_____小时之后到达_____机场。为了解除您旅途的疲劳，现在为您播放机上健康养生视频。视频结束后 10 分钟我们将为您提供_____(午餐/晚餐/早餐/小吃/快餐)。
谢谢！

6.2.4　Concluding the Duty-free Sales(停止出售免税品广播)

Ladies and gentlemen,
Due to time restriction, we have to conclude the duty-free sales in _____ minutes. Please let us know if you are interested in making a purchase.
Thank you!

女士们，先生们：
由于时间的限制，我们将于_____分钟后停止出售免税品。如您仍想购买，请尽快与我们联系。
谢谢！

6.2.5　Spraying for Disinfection(喷药)

Ladies and gentlemen,
According to local government quarantine requirements, all incoming aircrafts must be sprayed for disinfection. We are using the disinfectant harmless to the human body. We will be briefly spraying the cabin in a minute.

女士们，先生们：
根据当地检疫部门的要求，所有进港飞机必须喷雾消毒。我们使用的消毒剂对人体无害。我们将在一分钟内完成喷药。

Announcements Part III

If you are sensitive to sprays, we suggest that you place your tissue over your nose and mouth while we pass by.

Passengers who wear contact lenses, please close your eyes during this process.

Thank you for your cooperation!

如果您对喷雾过敏，请您在工作人员路过时，用纸巾捂住口鼻。

佩戴隐形眼镜的旅客，请在这一过程中闭上眼睛。

感谢您的合作。

6.2.6 20/30 Minutes Prior to Landing(着陆前 20/30 分钟)

Ladies and gentlemen,

We will be arriving at _____ airport in 20/30 minutes. There is a(an) _____-hour time difference between _____ and _____. The local time in _____ is _____ A.M./P.M. on _____(date). The temperature is _____ degrees Centigrade or _____ degrees Fahrenheit.

As the outside temperature is relatively high (low), we suggest you take off (put on) your clothing when you disembark.

As we prepare for landing, please return your seatback to the upright position, secure your table and footrest, open the window shades and check that your seat belt is securely fastened. All electronic devices must be switched off at this time. You must not turn on mobile phones until the seat belt sign is switched off.

We are about to dim the cabin light. If you would like to read, we suggest you use your reading light.

Thank you!

女士们，先生们：

本架飞机大约在 20/30 分钟后到达_____机场，与_____的时差为_____小时。现在是_____(到达站)时间星期_____上午/下午_____点_____分。温度为_____摄氏度或_____华氏度。

由于机舱内外温差较大，我们提醒您当您下机时适当减少(增加)衣服。

飞机已经开始下降，请您调直座椅靠背，收起小桌板及脚踏板，打开遮光板并系好安全带。为了避免干扰驾驶舱内的飞行仪器，请关闭所有电子设备，在舱门开启前请您不要打开手机。

稍后我们将调暗灯光，需要阅读的旅客，建议您打开阅读灯。

谢谢！

6.2.7　Farewell and Giving Regards(着陆前致意)

Ladies and gentlemen,
On behalf of the entire crew, we would like to thank you for your support and cooperation during the flight.
Thank you!

女士们，先生们：
对您在旅途中给予的支持和帮助，我们全体机组成员表示最诚挚的谢意。
谢谢！

6.2.8　Video Demonstration of the Transit Procedures (视频演示中转流程)

Ladies and gentlemen,
All transit passengers, may I have your attention please? We have a video on your transit. We hope it helps.
Thank you!

女士们，先生们：
为了方便您办理转乘手续，现在为您播放中转航班信息。希望对您有所帮助。
谢谢！

6.2.9　Announcement of Transit Flights(中转航班通告)

Ladies and gentlemen,
All transit passengers, may I have your attention please? This is the announcement about your transfer flights.
Passengers to _____ on CA_____, please proceed to the boarding gate _____.
Passengers to _____ on CA_____, please proceed to the boarding gate _____.
Passengers transferring to international flights with baggage that has been checked to the final destination, please proceed to the transit counter directly.

女士们，先生们：
所有中转航班的旅客们，请注意，下面向您播报中转航班信息。

经北京中转前往_____的旅客，您乘坐的 CA_____航班，登机口在_____号。
前往_____的旅客，您乘坐的 CA_____航班，登机口在_____号。
转乘国际航班，且已办理行李联运的旅客，请直接前往国航中转服务柜台办理转乘手续。

Announcements Part III

Passengers transferring to domestic flights, according to customs regulations, you have to claim your checked baggage first for customs clearance, and then, proceed to the transit counter. All your checked baggage will be arriving at carousel No. _____

If your final destination is Beijing, you may also claim your checked baggage at baggage carousel No. _____

Thank you!

转乘国内航班的旅客，根据海关规定，您必须在北京机场提取行李，办理海关查验手续，然后前往国航中转服务柜台办理行李再托运手续，托运行李请在_____号传送带提取。

终点站为北京的旅客，请您同样在_____号传送带提取托运行李。

谢谢！

Words and Expressions

blanket ['blæŋkɪt] *n.* 毛毯，毯子

lower ['ləʊə] *adj.* 较低的；下方的
　　　　　　vt. & vi. 降低；减少

shade [ʃeɪd] *n.* 遮阳；百叶窗；窗帘

window shade　窗帘

duty ['dju:tɪ] *n.* 职责；税

merchandise ['mɜ:tʃəndaɪz] *n.* 商品；货物

accompany [əˈkʌmpəni] *vt.* 陪伴，陪同；附有

receipt [rɪˈsi:t] *n.* 收据，收条；收入

seal [sil] *n.* 印章；海豹；封条
　　　v. 密封；封盖……的表面；封上(信封)

book [bʊk] *vt. & vi.* 预订

in case　假使；以防万一

specify ['spesɪfaɪ] *vt.* 具体指明；详述

fitness ['fɪtnɪs] *n.* 健康；适当

due to　因为；由于

restriction [rɪˈstrɪkʃən] *n.* 限制，限定

make a purchase　选购

conclude [kənˈkluːd] *vi.* 结束，终止；
　　　　　　　　　　vt. 得出结论；缔结；结束，终止
spray [spreɪ] *vt.* 喷；喷洒
　　　　　　　n. 喷雾，喷剂
disinfect [ˌdɪsɪnˈfekt] *vt.* 为……消毒，给……杀菌
sensitive [ˈsensɪtɪv] *adj.* 敏感的
contact lens [ˈkɒnˌtækt lenz] *n.* 接触镜；隐形眼镜
tissue [ˈtɪsjuː] *n.* 薄纸，棉纸；纸巾，面巾纸

6.3　Prior to Landing(落地前)

6.3.1　Seat Belt Fastened(确认系好安全带)

Ladies and gentlemen,
　　Our plane will be landing shortly. Please confirm that your seat belt is securely fastened.
　　Thank you!

女士们，先生们：
　　我们的飞机马上就要着陆了。请您再次确认系好您的安全带。

　　谢谢！

6.3.2　Terminal Landing(终点着陆)

Ladies and gentlemen,
　　We have just arrived in _____ airport Terminal _____.
　　There is a(an) _____-hour time difference between _____ and _____. The local time in _____ is _____ A.M./P.M. on _____(date). The temperature is _____ degrees Centigrade or _____ degrees Fahrenheit.

女士们，先生们：
　　我们已经到达_____机场，您将在_____号候机楼办理手续。_____与_____的时差为_____。现在是_____(到达站)时间星期_____上午/下午_____点_____分。机舱外的温度为_____摄氏度_____华氏度。

Announcements   Part III

Our plane is taxiing, Please remain seated with your seat belt fastened and luggage stowed. The use of mobile phone is prohibited until the seat belt sign is switched off. And we remind you to use caution when opening the overhead compartments. Please take all your belongings with you when you disembark.

Passengers arrived in _____, please claim your checked baggage and proceed to entry procedures.

All transit passengers, please proceed to the transit lounge.

Passengers from _____, please proceed to the international lounge to complete customs procedures.

Passengers from _____, please proceed to domestic lounge.

We apologize for your trip impact of fight delays. Highly appreciated for your patience and understanding during the waiting time.

Thank you for flying Air China, a member of the Star Alliance network. We hope you'll enjoy your stay in _____.

Good-bye!

飞机还将滑行一段距离，在安全带指示灯熄灭以前，请您系好安全带，在座位上耐心等候。在此期间，请不要打开手机。请小心开启行李架，以免行李滑落。下机时，请您带好所有随身物品。

到达_____的旅客，请在本站办理检疫、入境及海关手续。

所有过境旅客，请到中转柜台办理中转手续。

由_____到达本站的旅客，请走国际厅，办理海关手续。

由_____到达本站的旅客，请走国内厅。

由于航班延误，影响了您的行程，我们深表歉意。对于您在等待时所表现出的耐心与理解，我们深表感谢！

感谢您选乘星空联盟成员中国国际航空公司航班，我们期待与您下次旅途再会，祝您在_____愉快！

再见！

6.3.3 International-domestic Connecting(国内经停)

Ladies and gentlemen,

We have just arrived in _____ airport Terminal _____.

There is a(an) _____-hour time difference between _____ and _____. The local time in _____ is _____A.M./P.M. on _____(date).

女士们，先生们：

我们已经到达_____机场，您将在_____号候机楼进港或办理手续。

_____与_____的时差为_____小时，现在是_____(到达站)时间为星期_____上午/下午_____点_____分。

The temperature is _____ degrees Centigrade or _____ degrees Fahrenheit.

Please remain seated with your seat belt fastened and luggage stowed. The use of mobile phone is prohibited until the seat belt sign is switched off. And please use caution when opening the overhead compartments.

For outbound passengers arrived in _____, please claim your checked baggage. For all transit passengers, please proceed to the transit lounge.

Passengers continuing to _____, please disembark with all your belongings and proceed to exit formalities. Please keep aware of the boarding time.

For inbound passengers arrived in _____, please proceed to entry proce-dures. For all transit passengers, please proceed to the transit lounge.

Passengers, continuing on to _____, please disembark with all your belongings and go through the immigration and quarantine formalities. Customs procedures will be completed at _____(destination). Wait for your boarding call and get on board on time.

Highly appreciated for your patience and understanding during the waiting time.

We will change crew here.

I represent the crew of the flight to thank you for flying Air China, a member of the Star Alliance network. We hope you'll enjoy your stay in _____!

Good-bye!

机舱外的温度为_____摄氏度_____华氏度。

飞机还将滑行一段距离，在安全带指示灯熄灭以前，请您系好安全带，在座位上耐心等候。在此期间，请不要打开手机。下机时请小心开启行李架，以免行李滑落。

(去程)到达_____的旅客，请在本站领取交运行李。如果您需转乘其他航班，请到中转柜台办理中转手续。

搭乘本次航班继续前往_____的旅客，请带好全部手提物品下飞机，在本站办理出境手续。请您在候机室休息，等候广播通知上飞机。

(回程)到达_____的旅客，请在本站办理入境手续。如果您需要转乘其他航班，请到中转柜台办理中转手续。

搭乘本次航班继续前往_____的旅客，请带好全部手提物品下飞机，在本站办理入境及检疫手续。海关手续在_____(终点站)办理。请您在候机室休息，等候广播通知上飞机。

对于您在等待时所表现出的耐心与理解，我们深表感谢！

我们将在这里更换机组。

我谨代表全体机组成员感谢您选乘星空联盟成员中国国际航空公司航班，我们期待与您下次旅途再会，祝您在_____愉快！

再见！

6.3.4 International Connecting(国际经停)

Ladies and gentlemen,

We have just arrived in _____ airport Terminal _____.

There is a(an) _____-hour time difference between _____ and _____. The local time in _____ is _____ (AM/PM) on _____(date).

The temperature is_____degrees Centigrade or _____ degrees Fahrenheit.

Our plane is taxiing. Please remain seated with your seat belt fastened and luggage stowed. The use of mobile phone is prohibited until the seat belt sign is switched off. And we remind you to use caution when opening the overhead compartments.

Passengers for _____, please claim your checked baggage and go through the immigration. All transit passengers, please proceed to the transit lounge.

Passengers continuing on to _____, go through the immigration after your arrival at your destination.

Please take all your belongings with you and disembark. Wait for your boarding call and get on board on time.

Highly appreciated for your patience and understanding during the waiting time.

We will change crew here.

Thank you for flying Air China, a member of the Star Alliance network. We hope you'll enjoy your stay in_____.

Good-bye!

女士们,先生们:

我们已经到达_____机场,您将在_____号候机楼进港或办理手续。

_____与_____的时差为_____小时,现在是_____(到达站)时间星期_____(上午/下午)_____点_____分。

机舱外的温度是_____摄氏度_____华氏度。

我们的飞机还将滑行一段距离。在安全带指示灯熄灭以前,请您系好安全带,在座位上耐心等候。在此期间,请不要打开手机。下机时请小心开启行李架,以免行李滑落。

到达_____的旅客,请在本站办理检疫、入境及海关手续,并到国际大厅领取您的托运行李。如果您需转乘其他航班,请到中转柜台办理中转手续。

继续搭乘本次航班前往_____的旅客,请带上您的全部物品下机,并在候机楼休息,您无须在本站办理入境手续。登机时我们会广播通知您。

对于您在等待时所表现出的耐心与理解,我们深表感谢!

我们将在这里更换机组。

我谨代表全体机组成员感谢您选乘星空联盟成员中国国际航空公司航班,我们期待与您下次旅途再会,祝您在_____愉快!

再见!

6.3.5 International Connecting-PAX(国际经停，旅客机上等候)

Ladies and gentlemen,

We have just arrived in _____ airport Terminal _____.

There is a(an) _____-hour time difference between _____ and _____. The local time in _____ is _____A.M./P.M. on _____(date). The temperature is _____ degrees Centigrade or _____ degrees Fahrenheit.

Our plane is taxiing. Please remain seated with your seat belt fastened and luggage stowed. The use of mobile phone is prohibited until the seat belt sign is switched off. And we remind you to use caution when opening the overhead compartments.

Passengers for _____, please claim your checked baggage and go through the immigration. All transit passengers, please proceed to the transit lounge.

Passengers continuing on to _____, you are required to remain on board during the stopover. We ask you to return to your original seat so that we can clean the cabin.

Highly appreciated for your patience and understanding during the waiting time.

We will change crew here.

Thank you for flying Air China, a member of the Star Alliance network. We hope you'll enjoy your stay in _____.

Good-bye!

女士们，先生们：

我们已经到达_____机场，飞机将停靠在_____号候机楼。

_____与_____的时差为_____小时，现在是_____(到达站)时间星期_____上午/下午_____点_____分。机舱外的温度为_____摄氏度_____华氏度。

我们的飞机还将滑行一段距离。在安全带指示灯熄灭以前，请您系好安全带，在座位上耐心等候。在此期间，请不要打开手机。下机时请小心开启行李架，以免行李滑落。

到达_____的旅客，请到候机楼办理检疫、入境及海关手续。如果您需转乘其他航班，请到中转柜台办理中转手续。

继续搭乘本次航班前往_____的旅客，请您在原位休息等候，我们将进行客舱准备工作，请您予以配合。

对于您在等待时所表现出的耐心与理解，我们深表感谢！

我们将在这里更换机组。

我谨代表全体机组成员感谢您选乘星空联盟成员中国国际航空公司航班，我们期待与您下次旅途再会，祝您在_____愉快！

再见！

Words and Expressions

lounge [laʊndʒ] *n.* 休息厅；客厅；(机场的)等候室
claim [kleɪm] *vt.* 声称；断言；需要；索取
outbound [ˈaʊtˌbaʊnd] *adj.* 开往外地的，开往外国的
proceed [prəˈsiːd] *vi.* 继续进行，继续做；(沿特定路线)行进
keep aware of 意识到
inbound [ˈɪnˌbaʊnd] *adj.* 回内地的；归本国的；到达的；入境的
boarding call 最后登机广播

Practice

Ⅰ. Look and Say

Tell the words according to the given pictures, both in English and in Chinese.

1

2

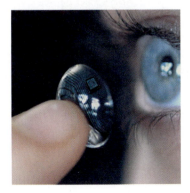

3

4

5

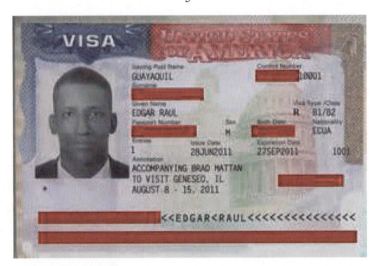

6

7

Ⅱ. Word Matching

Match the words in Column A with their definitions in Column B.

1

Column A

citizen
distribute
immigrant
mainland
submit
incoming
holder
overseas
waiver

Column B

(1) hand over formally(提交，递呈)

(2) the principal landmass of a continent(大陆：大洲的主要陆地板块)

(3) a person who has the legal right to belong to a particular country(公民：具有或取得某国国籍，并根据宪法和法律规定享有权利和承担相应义务的人)

(4) to divide and dispense in portions(分发，分配，分给)

(5) a person who leaves one country to settle permanently in another(移民：离开自己的国家并到别国永久定居的人)

(6) intentional relinquishment of a right, claim, or privilege(放弃：自动地放弃一项权利、主张或特权)

(7) coming in or about to come in; entering(进来的，到来的：将要或正要进来的；进入的)

(8) one that possesses something; an owner(拥有者：拥有某物的人；物主)

(9) beyond the sea; abroad(在海外或向海外)

2

Column A

specify
accompany
spray
purchase
available
receipt
dim
duty
blanket
destination

Column B

(1) the place to which one is going or directed(目的地：一个人要到达的地方)

(2) lacking in brightness(不明亮的)

(3) a fine jet of liquid discharged from a pressurized container(喷雾：从一个加有压力的容器中向外喷射的细雾)

(4) to state explicitly or in detail(明确说明或详细指明)

(5) a written acknowledgment that a specified article, sum of money, or shipment of merchandise has been received(证据：表明证实某具体物件、钱款或商业货物已接到的书面证据)

(6) taxes which you pay to the government on goods that you buy(税收)

(7) a large piece of woven material used as a covering for warmth, especially on a bed(毛毯：羊毛制的用于取暖的一大块覆盖物，尤指用于床上)

(8) present and ready for use; at hand; accessible(可用的：现实可用的；手边的；可获得的)

(9) to obtain in exchange for money or its equivalent; buy(购买：通过交换货币或其等价物而得到；买)

(10) to be or go with as a companion(陪伴，陪同：作为同伴相处或同行)

3

Column A

claim
behalf
lounge
proceed
outbound
shortly
formalities
aware
secure
inbound

Column B

(1) bound inward; incoming(归航的；开回的)

(2) to go forward or onward, especially after an interruption; continue(继续进行：进行或前进，尤指被打断后继续进行；继续)

(3) outward bound; headed away(向外去的；向外开的)

(4) having knowledge or consciousness(意识到的或认识到的)

(5) a public waiting room, as in a hotel or an air terminal, often having smoking or lavatory facilities(休息室：一间公共的等候室，比如在宾馆里或飞机终点，一般有吸烟或卫生设备)

(6) in a short time; soon(立刻；马上)

(7) interest, support, or benefit(利益、支持或好处)

(8) free from danger or attack(安全的：没有危险或免受攻击的)

(9) to demand or ask for as one's own or one's due; assert one's right to(主张，要求：要求或寻求……归为己有；维护自己对……的权利)

(10) formal actions or procedures that are carried out as part of a particular activity or event(正式手续)

III. Announcement Completion

Fill in the blanks with words or expressions given, and then work in pairs to read aloud to each other.

Announcement 1

arrival	landing	declaration	entry	passport
required	available	programs	explaining	traveling

Ladies and gentlemen,

  We will now distribute immigration and customs forms. The United States government requires that the landing form be completed by all passengers before ___(1)___ . U.S. ___(2)___ holders, immigrants, Green Card holders or Canadian citizens do not need to complete the ___(3)___ forms. Passengers who are entering the United States under the Non-Immigrant Visa Waiver ___(4)___ should complete the form which is also ___(5)___ .

  Besides, all passengers are ___(6)___ to complete U.S. customs ___(7)___ forms. Only one form is necessary for a family ___(8)___ together.

  We will now play a video ___(9)___ how to fill in the forms necessary for ___(10)___ into the United States.

  This is Air China flight CA817. If you have any difficulty completing the forms, please let us know.

Announcement 2

attention	domestic	transfer	flights	carousel
proceed	directly	checked	regulations	clearance

Ladies and gentlemen,

  All transit passengers, may I have your ___(1)___ please? This is the announcement about your ___(2)___ flights.

  Passengers to Beijing on CA982, please ___(3)___ to the boarding gate 10.

  Passengers transferring to international ___(4)___ with baggage that has been ___(5)___ to the final destination, please proceed to the transit counter ___(6)___ .

  Passengers transferring to ___(7)___ flights, according to customs ___(8)___ , you have to claim your checked baggage first for customs ___(9)___ , and then, proceed to the transit counter.

Announcements Part III

All your checked baggage will be arriving at carousel No. 3.

If your final destination is Beijing, you may also claim your checked baggage at ___(10)___ No. 4.

Thank you!

Announcement 3

| appreciated | difference | caution | continuing | luggage |
| sign | immigration | overhead | local | terminal |

Ladies and gentlemen,

We have just arrived in Tokyo airport ___(1)___ 3.

There is a one-hour time ___(2)___ between Beijing and Tokyo. The ___(3)___ time in Tokyo is 9:35 A.M. on 26th July.

The temperature is 26 degrees Centigrade or 78.8 degrees Fahrenheit.

Please remain seated with your seat belt fastened and ___(4)___ stowed. The use of mobile phone is prohibited until the seat belt ___(5)___ is switched off. And we remind you to use ___(6)___ when opening the ___(7)___ compartments.

Passengers for Tokyo, please claim your checked baggage and go through the ___(8)___. All transit passengers, please proceed to the transit lounge. Passengers ___(9)___ on to Los Angeles, go through the immigration after your arrival at your destination.

Please take all your belongings with you and disembark. Wait for your boarding call and get on board on time.

Highly ___(10)___ for your patience and understanding during the waiting time.

We will change crew here.

Thank you for flying Air China, a member of the Star Alliance network. We hope you'll enjoy your stay in Tokyo.

Good-bye!

Ⅳ. Further Study

1. 出入境检验检疫报检规定

第一章　总则

第一条　为加强出入境检验检疫报检管理，规范报检行为，根据《中华人民共和国进出口商品检验法》及其实施条例、《中华人民共和国进出境动植物检疫法》及其实施条例、《中华人民共和国国境卫生检疫法》及其实施细则、《中华人民共和国食品卫生法》等法律法规的有关规定，制定本规定。

第二条　根据法律法规规定办理出入境检验检疫报检/申报的行为均适用本规定。

第三条　报检范围

(一)国家法律法规规定必须由出入境检验检疫机构(以下简称检验检疫机构)检验检疫的。

(二)输入国家或地区规定必须凭检验检疫机构出具的证书方准入境的。

(三)有关国际条约规定须经检验检疫的。

(四)申请签发原产地证明书及普惠制原产地证明书的。

第四条　报检人在报检时应填写规定格式的报检单，提供与出入境检验检疫有关的单证资料，按规定交纳检验检疫费。

第五条　报检单填制要求

(一)报检人须按要求填写报检单所列内容；书写工整、字迹清晰，不得涂改；报检日期按检验检疫机构受理报检日期填写。

(二)报检单必须加盖报检单位印章。

第二章　报检资格

第六条　报检单位首次报检时须持本单位营业执照和政府批文办理登记备案手续，取得报检单位代码。其报检人员经检验检疫机构培训合格后领取"报检员证"，凭证报检。

第七条　代理报检单位须按规定办理注册登记手续，其报检人员经检验检疫机构培训合格后领取"代理报检员证"，凭证办理代理报检手续。

第八条　代理报检的，须向检验检疫机构提供委托书，委托书由委托人按检验检疫机构规定的格式填写。

第九条　非贸易性质的报检行为，报检人凭有效证件可直接办理报检手续。

第三章　入境报检

第十条　入境报检时，应填写入境货物报检单并提供合同、发票、提单等有关单证。

第十一条　下列情况报检时除按第十条规定办理外，还应按要求提供有关文件。

(一)凡实施安全质量许可、卫生注册或其他需审批审核的货物，应提供有关证明。

(二)品质检验的还应提供国外品质证书或质量保证书、产品使用说明书及有关标准和技术资料；凭样成交的，须加附成交样品；以品级或公量计价结算的，应同时申请重量鉴定。

(三)报检入境废物时，还应提供国家环保部门签发的《进口废物批准证书》和经认可的检验机构签发的装运前检验合格证书等。

(四)申请残损鉴定的还应提供理货残损单、铁路商务记录、空运事故记录或海事报告等证明货损情况的有关单证。

(五)申请重(数)量鉴定的还应提供重量明细单、理货清单等。

(六)货物经收、用货部门验收或其他单位检测的,应随附验收报告或检测结果以及重量明细单等。

(七)入境的国际旅行者,应填写入境检疫申明卡。

(八)入境的动植物及其产品,在提供贸易合同、发票、产地证书的同时,还必须提供输出国家或地区官方的检疫证书;需办理入境检疫审批手续的,还应提供入境动植物检疫许可证。

(九)过境动植物及其产品报检时,应持货运单和输出国家或地区官方出具的检疫证书;运输动物过境时,还应提交国家检验检疫局签发的动植物过境许可证。

(十)报检入境运输工具、集装箱时,应提供检疫证明,并申报有关人员健康状况。

(十一)入境旅客、交通员工携带伴侣动物的,应提供入境动物检疫证书及预防接种证明。

(十二)因科研等特殊需要,输入禁止入境物的,必须提供国家检验检疫局签发的特许审批证明。

(十三)入境特殊物品的,应提供有关的批件或规定的文件。

第四章 出境报检

第十二条 出境报检时,应填写出境货物报检单并提供对外贸易合同(售货确认书或函电)、信用证、发票、装箱单等必要的单证。

第十三条 下列情况报检时除按第十二条规定办理外,还应按要求提供有关文件。

(一)凡实施质量许可、卫生注册或需经审批的货物,应提供有关证明。

(二)出境货物须经生产者或经营者检验合格并加附检验合格证或检测报告;申请重量鉴定的,应加附重量明细单或磅码单。

(三)凭样成交的货物,应提供经买卖双方确认的样品。

(四)出境人员应向检验检疫机构申请办理国际旅行健康证明书及国际预防接种证书。

(五)报检出境运输工具、集装箱时,还应提供检疫证明,并申报有关人员健康状况。

(六)生产出境危险货物包装容器的企业,必须向检验检疫机构申请包装容器的性能鉴定。生产出境危险货物的企业,必须向检验检疫机构申请危险货物包装容器的使用鉴定。

(七)报检出境危险货物时,必须提供危险货物包装容器性能鉴定结果单和使用鉴定结果单。

(八)申请原产地证明书和普惠制原产地证明书的,应提供商业发票等资料。

(九)出境特殊物品的,根据法律法规规定应提供有关的审批文件。

第五章　报检及证单的更改

第十四条　报检人申请撤销报检时，应书面说明原因，经批准后方可办理撤销手续。

第十五条　报检后 30 天内未联系检验检疫事宜的，作自动撤销报检处理。

第十六条　有下列情况之一的应重新报检：

(一)超过检验检疫有效期限的；

(二)变更输入国家或地区，并又有不同检验检疫要求的；

(三)改换包装或重新拼装的；

(四)已撤销报检的。

第十七条　报检人申请更改证单时，应填写更改申请单，交附有关函电等证明单据，并交还原证单，经审核同意后方可办理更改手续。品名、数(重)量、检验检疫结果、包装、发货人、收货人等重要项目更改后与合同、信用证不符的，或者更改后与输出、输入国家或地区法律法规规定不符的，均不能更改。

第六章　报检时限和地点

第十八条　对入境货物，应在入境前或入境时向入境口岸、指定的或到达站的检验检疫机构办理报检手续；入境的运输工具及人员应在入境前或入境时申报。

第十九条　入境货物需对外索赔出证的，应在索赔有效期前不少于 20 天内向到货口岸或货物到达地的检验检疫机构报检。

第二十条　输入微生物、人体组织、生物制品、血液及其制品或种畜、禽及其精液、胚胎、受精卵的，应当在入境前 30 天报检。

第二十一条　输入其他动物的，应当在入境前 15 天报检。

第二十二条　输入植物、种子、种苗及其他繁殖材料的，应当在入境前 7 天报检。

第二十三条　出境货物最迟应于报关或装运前 7 天报检，对于个别检验检疫周期较长的货物，应留有相应的检验检疫时间。

第二十四条　出境的运输工具和人员应在出境前向口岸检验检疫机构报检或申报。

第二十五条　需隔离检疫的出境动物在出境前 60 天预报，隔离前 7 天报检。

第二十六条　报检人对检验检疫证单有特殊要求的，应在报检单上注明并交付相关文件。

第七章　附则

第二十七条　报检单位和报检人伪造、买卖、变造、涂改、盗用检验检疫机构的证单、印章的，按有关法律法规予以处罚。

第二十八条　司法鉴定业务、行政机关委托及其他委托检验和鉴定业务，参照本规定执行。

第二十九条　本规定由国家出入境检验检疫局负责解释。

第三十条 本规定自 2000 年 1 月 1 日起施行，原国家商检局发布的《进出口商品报验规定》和原国家卫生检疫局发布的《关于对入、出境集装箱、货物实行报检制度的通知》同时废止。

2. 绿卡

绿卡(Green Card)是一种给外国公民的永久居住许可证。持有绿卡意味着持卡人拥有在签发国的永久居留权。同时，持有绿卡可以在一定时间内免去入境签证。绿卡这个词起源于美国，因为最早的美国永久居留许可证是一张绿色的卡片。虽然后来随着设计风格的变化该卡片已更新了 20 多个版本，但是绿卡这个名称却被一直保留了下来。2010 年 5 月美国的绿卡又重新变回了绿色，一改之前的白底加黄绿色花纹。由于其他国家沿用了美国的叫法，因此也将本国的永久居留许可证俗称为绿卡。

Unit 7　　Special Occasions Announcements

(特殊情况广播)

7.1　Brief Introduction(简要介绍)

7.1.1　Organizations(各类团体)

> Ladies and gentlemen,
> Welcome aboard Air China, a proud Star Alliance member. This is flight CA_____to _____.
> Traveling with us today are _____(group/delegates) attending the _____(name of event) in _____. On behalf of Air China, we wish you a successful meeting (convention/conference)!

> 女士们，先生们：
> 欢迎您选乘星空联盟成员中国国际航空公司_____航班前往_____。
> 同时我们也诚挚地欢迎_____(团队/代表)乘坐我们的飞机前往_____参加_____会议(活动)，我们衷心预祝会议(活动)取得圆满成功！

7.1.2　Maiden Flight(首航)

> Ladies and gentlemen,
> Good morning(afternoon/evening)!
> Welcome aboard the first flight of Air China, a proud Star Alliance, to _____, We are looking forward to giving you a perfect experience on board.
> The flying distance from _____ to _____ is _____ kilometers, and the flight will take _____ hour(s) and _____ minutes.

> 女士们，先生们：
> 早上(下午/晚上)好！
> 欢迎您乘坐星空联盟成员中国国际航空公司的首航航班前往_____，我们全体机组成员竭诚为您服务。
> 从_____至_____的空中飞行距离是_____。预计空中飞行时间为_____小时_____分钟。

Announcements Part III

We will be taking off soon. Please fasten your seat belt and confirm that your electronic devices such as mobile phones, have been switched off. Please do not smoke during the flight.

If you need any assistance, please let us know.

We hope you will enjoy the flight.

Thank you!

我们很快就要起飞了。请您系好安全带，关闭手机等电子设备，在整个旅途中请不要吸烟。

如果您需要帮助，请告知我们。

祝您旅途愉快！
谢谢！

7.1.3 Anniversary of Air China(中国国际航空周年纪念日)

Good morning(afternoon/evening), ladies and gentlemen!

Captain _____ and his crew would like to welcome you aboard Air China, a proud Star Alliance member. This is a flight to _____. Today is the _____ anniversary of our airlines. On this special day, we feel delighted to have you on board.

On our flight today, there are _____ flight attendants at your service. We wish you a pleasant flight!

Thank you!

女士们，先生们，早上(下午/晚上)好！

_____机长和全体乘务员欢迎您乘坐星空联盟成员中国国际航空公司航班前往_____。今天是中国国际航空公司成立_____周年的纪念日，在今天这个特别的日子里，能与您相逢在蓝天，我们全体机组成员感到非常高兴。

在本次航班上有_____名乘务员，我们将为您提供及时周到的服务。祝各位旅途愉快！

谢谢！

7.1.4 Merged Flights(合并航班)

Ladies and gentlemen,

Welcome aboard Air China, a member of the Star Alliance network flight CA_____ and CA_____ from _____ to _____.

女士们，先生们：

欢迎您选乘星空联盟成员中国国际航空公司CA_____和CA_____航班从_____前往_____。

We feel grateful to all passengers and Phoenix Miles members for your business, and you are very much welcome to join the Phoenix Miles, our frequent flyer program.

As we are preparing for take-off, please fasten your seat belt, switch off your mobile phone and any kind of electronic devices.

We will now play you a video explaining the safety features of the aircraft. We hope you will enjoy the flight and wish you a pleasant journey.

Thank you!

非常感谢各位旅客、国航知音会员长期以来对国航的支持与信赖，真诚邀请更多旅客加入国航常旅客计划。

飞机即将起飞，请您系好安全带，并关闭手机等电子设备。

现在为您播放安全须知录像，请留意收看。我们全体机组成员将竭诚为您服务，祝您旅途愉快。

谢谢！

7.1.5 Take-off(中途起飞)

Ladies and gentlemen,

Welcome aboard Air China, a Star Alliance member, flight CA_____ to _____.

We feel grateful to all passengers and Phoenix Miles members for your business, and you are very much welcome to join the Phoenix Miles, our frequent flyer program.

As we are preparing for take-off, please fasten your seat belt, switch off your mobile phone and any kind of electronic devices.

We will now play you a video explaining the safety features of the aircraft. We hope you will enjoy the flight and wish you a pleasant journey.

Thank you!

女士们，先生们：

欢迎您继续选乘从_____飞往_____的星空联盟成员中国国际航空公司航班。

非常感谢各位旅客、国航知音会员长期以来对国航的支持与信赖，真诚邀请更多旅客加入国航常旅客计划。

飞机即将起飞，请您系好安全带，并关闭手机等电子设备。

现在为您播放安全须知录像，请留意收看。

我们全体机组成员将竭诚为您服务，祝您旅途愉快。

谢谢！

Words and Expressions

maiden [ˈmeɪdn] *adj.* 处女的,少女的;首次的,初次的

maiden flight 首航

anniversary [ˌænɪˈvɜːsərɪ] *n.* 周年纪念日

merge [mɜːdʒ] *vt. & vi.* (使)混合;相融;融入

merged flights 合并航班

7.2　In the Cabin(舱内情况)

7.2.1　Prior to Door Closing(关舱门登机前)

Ladies and gentlemen,

Welcome aboard Air China, a proud Star Alliance member. Before we depart, your luggage must be stowed in an overhead compartment or under the seat in front of you.

Please step out of the aisle and into your row as quickly as possible so that other passengers are able to reach their seats.

Thank you!

女士们,先生们:

欢迎您选乘星空联盟成员中国国际航空公司航班。在我们出发前,务必请将您的行李放在行李架内或您前面座椅下。

请您让开廊道,尽快入座,以方便后面的旅客登机。

谢谢!

7.2.2　Picking up Duty-free Merchandise(领取免税品)

Ladies and gentlemen,

Please pick up your duty-free merchandise at the boarding gate.

Thank you!

女士们,先生们:
请到登机门处领取免税商品。

谢谢!

7.2.3 Head Count(清点旅客)

Ladies and gentlemen,

We are requested to take a count of all passengers on board. Please remain in your seat and refrain from using the lavatories during this process.

Thank you!

女士们，先生们：

现在我们需要重新核对旅客人数。请您协助我们在座位上坐好，卫生间暂停使用。

谢谢！

7.2.4 Passengers Cancel Journey(因旅客临时取消航班而清舱)

Ladies and gentlemen,

Now the security agents will check our aircraft again because some passengers have cancelled their flights. So please disembark with all your belongings and follow the ground staff's directions. Please check the pocket in front of you and confirm that there are no personal items left before getting off.

Thank you for your cooperation.

Thank you!

女士们，先生们：

现在，由于部分旅客临时取消航班，为了确保所有旅客的安全，我们的飞机将重新进行安全检查。请所有旅客带好您的全部物品，并检查座椅前面的口袋，确认没有遗忘任何个人物品后再下机。

感谢您的配合。

谢谢！

7.2.5 Temporarily Adjusting Seats(临时调整座位)

Ladies and gentlemen,

In order to keep the aircraft in a better balance, the occupation of seats will be adjusted temporarily.

Please follow the direction of the flight attendants.

You may take your booked seats after take-off.

Thank you for your cooperation!

女士们,先生们:

为了保持飞机的平衡,将暂时调整座位。

请按乘务员指示调整座位。

飞机起飞后再坐回原位。

感谢您的合作!

7.2.6 Auxiliary Power Supply Failure and Increase of Cabin Temperature(APU 故障,客舱温度过高)

Ladies and gentlemen,

We are sorry to inform you that due to the auxiliary power supply failure, air conditioning does not function properly on the ground. We have already informed the relevant departments for ground support equipment, and cabin temperature will gradually decrease. We will provide you with more details as soon as they become available. We will now offer beverages.

Thank you for your understanding and cooperation!

女士们,先生们:

我们非常遗憾地通知您,由于辅助动力电源失效,飞机在地面等待期间无法启用空调系统。我们已经通知相关部门调用地面辅助设备,客舱温度将会逐步降低。进一步的消息,我们会及时广播通知您。现在我们将为您提供饮料。

感谢您的理解与合作!

7.2.7　Delay in Departure(延误起飞)

Ladies and gentlemen,
　　Our departure will be postponed _____ hours/minutes due to _____.
　　Please remain in your seat. We will provide more details as soon as we get further information. We will now offer beverages(breakfast/lunch/supper).
　　Thank you for your understanding and cooperation!

女士们，先生们：
　　由于_____(原因)，我们的航班将推迟起飞_____小时/分钟左右。
　　请各位旅客在座位上休息等候。进一步的消息，我们会及时通知您。现在客舱乘务员将为您提供饮料(早餐/午餐/晚餐)。
　　感谢您的理解与配合！

7.2.8　Delay (Congestion)[延误(飞机排队等待起飞)]

Ladies and gentlemen,
　　We are still waiting for the take-off clearance. There are _____ aircrafts lining up ahead of us. Please remain seated with your seat belt fastened until further notice.
　　Thank you!

女士们，先生们：
　　我们正在等待起飞的命令。我们现在排在第_____位。请您在座位上休息等候。

　　谢谢！

7.2.9　Extended Delay(继续延误)

Ladies and gentlemen,
　　We have been informed that due to _____, we'll still have to wait _____ minutes. We will provide more details as soon as we get further information.
　　We will now offer beverages(breakfast/lunch/supper).
　　Thank you for your understanding!

女士们，先生们：
　　由于_____原因，飞机还将继续等待_____分钟。进一步的消息，我们会及时通知您。

　　现在我们将为您提供饮料(早餐/午餐/晚餐)。
　　谢谢您的理解！

7.2.10 Having All Passengers Rest and Wait in the Terminal (回候机室休息)

Ladies and gentlemen,

We have been informed that our aircraft can not take off temporarily due to _____. We've decided to have all passengers to rest and wait in the terminal.

Thank you for your understanding and cooperation!

女士们，先生们：

我们刚刚收到通知，由于_____原因，飞机暂时不能起飞。我们决定安排大家到候机室休息等候。

感谢您的理解与配合！

7.2.11 Changing Aircraft(换乘飞机)

Ladies and gentlemen,

We are sorry that we will have to change to another aircraft due to technical problem. Please disembark with all your belongings and follow the direction of our ground staff.

Thank you for your understanding and cooperation!

女士们，先生们：

我们很抱歉，由于技术故障，我们不得不换乘另一架飞机。请您带好全部行李物品下飞机，听从我们地勤服务人员的安排。

感谢您的理解与配合！

7.2.12 Cancelled Flight(航班取消)

Ladies and gentlemen,

We have been informed that this flight has been cancelled due to _____(bad weather/technical trouble).

Please take all your belongings with you, check the pocket in front of you and confirm there are no personal items left before getting off. Our ground staff will provide you with further information.

女士们，先生们：

我们已获悉，由于_____(恶劣的天气/技术问题)取消了本次航班。

请所有旅客带好全部手提物品，并检查您座椅前面的口袋，确认没有遗忘任何个人物品后再下机。我们的地勤服务人员将为您提供最新的消息。

> We do apologize for the inconvenience and appreciate your understanding.
>
> Thank you!

> 由此带来的不便，我们深表歉意，感谢您的理解。
>
> 谢谢！

7.2.13 Safety Check(安全检查)

> Ladies and gentlemen,
>
> The airplane is taxiing into the runway for take-off. Flight attendants will start safety checks. Please return your seatback to the upright position, secure your table and footrest, open the window shades and check that your seat belt is securely fastened. All electronic devices must be switched off at this time.
>
> Thank you for your cooperation!

> 女士们，先生们：
>
> 飞机已经滑行准备起飞。客舱乘务员将进行安全检查。请您调直座椅靠背，收起小桌板和脚架，打开遮光板，系好安全带并关闭手机等所有电子设备。
>
> 感谢您的配合！

7.2.14 Taxiing(滑行)

> Ladies and gentlemen,
>
> Our airplane is taxiing, and all passengers must be seated with your seat belt fastened and luggage stowed.
>
> Thank you for your cooperation!

> 女士们，先生们：
>
> 我们的飞机正在滑行，为了您的安全，请系好安全带，并关闭行李箱。
>
> 感谢您的配合！

7.2.15 Cabin Installations(客舱设备介绍)

> Ladies and gentlemen,
>
> For your comfort and safety during the flight how we are going to introduce you the use of cabin installations.

> 女士们，先生们：
>
> 为了您旅途的舒适与安全，现在我们向您介绍客舱设备的使用方法。

Our aircraft for today's flight is a Boeing(Airbus) _____. Your seatback can be adjusted by pressing the button on your armrest. The reading light, call button and air vents are located above your head.

The lavatory for first class passengers is in the front of the aircraft and lavatories for passengers in the main cabin are in the rear of the aircraft.

If you need any assistance, please let us know.

Thank you!

您乘坐的是波音(空中客车)_____型飞机。您的座椅靠背可以调节，调节时请按座椅扶手上的按钮。在您的座椅上方设有阅读灯、呼唤铃和通风孔。

头等舱的卫生间在飞机的前部，普通舱的卫生间在飞机的后部。

如您需要帮助，请告知我们。

谢谢！

7.2.16　Equipped with Telephone(卫星电话)

Ladies and gentlemen,

In addition, this aircraft is equipped with telephone and a fax machine for your convenience. Please let us know if you need any assistance.

We hope that you will enjoy our service.

Thank you!

女士们，先生们：

为了方便您的使用，本架飞机备有空中卫星电话及传真机。如果您需要使用，请与我们联系。

希望您满意我们为您精心安排的各项服务。

谢谢！

7.2.17　Immigration Form/Customs Form/Quarantine Regulations Form Unavailable on Board(机上未配备目的地入境卡、海关申报单、检疫申明卡)

Ladies and gentlemen,

As we don't have _____(country/region) immigration form/customs form/quarantine regulations form on board, we can't provide for you. Please go to the corresponding counter for the form and fill it in after arriving at the terminal building.

Thank you!

女士们，先生们：

由于本次航班没有配备_____(国家/地区)入境卡/海关申报单/检疫申明卡，我们无法为您提供。请您在到达候机楼后，前往办理相应手续的柜台索取并填写。

谢谢！

7.2.18 Video System Failure(视频系统故障)

Ladies and gentlemen,

We are sorry that the video system is not available on this flight. You may have a wide selection of audio programs. We sincerely apologize for the inconvenience.

Thank you for your understanding and cooperation!

女士们，先生们：

我们非常抱歉，本架飞机并未配备视频系统。您可以选听丰富的音乐节目。由此给您带来的不便，我们深表歉意。

感谢您的理解与配合！

7.2.19 Clogged Toilet(卫生间故障)

Ladies and gentlemen,

We are sorry to inform you that the left/right toilet in the front/middle/rear of this aircraft can not be used since it has been clogged (can not be used on the ground, but can be used normally in the air). It will take a long time to solve this problem. In order to ensure you arrive at your destination on time, the problem will be fixed after the flight. We sincerely apologize for the imconvenience.

Thank you for your understanding and cooperation!

女士们，先生们：

我们很抱歉地通知您，由于本架飞机前/中/后部，左/右侧卫生间马桶堵塞，无法使用(地面停留期间无法使用，但在空中可以正常使用)。排除此故障，需要较长时间。为了保障您按时抵达目的地，故障将待航后排除。由此给您带来的不便，我们深表歉意。

感谢您的理解与支持！

Words and Expressions

cancel [ˈkænsəl] *vt.* 取消；撤销；废除

take count of 计数

temporarily [ˈtempərərɪlɪ] *adv.* 暂时地；一时半刻

adjust [əˈdʒʌst] *vt. & vi.* 适应，调整，校正；(使)习惯

keep balance 保持平衡

auxiliary [ɔɡˈzɪljəri] *adj.* 辅助的；备用的，补充的
auxiliary power 辅助动力电源
failure [ˈfeɪljə] *n.* 失败，故障，不及格；破产，倒闭
cabin temperature 客舱温度
air conditioning 空气调节装置；冷气
function [ˈfʌŋkʃən] *n.* 功能，作用；
　　　　　　　　 vi. 起作用；运作，运转
department [dɪˈpɑːtmənt] *n.* 部门，部；系，学部
relevant departments 相关部门
ground support equipment 地面保障设备，地面辅助设备
decrease [dɪˈkriːs] *n.* 减少；减少量
　　　　　　　　 vi. & vt. 减少，变小
postpone [pəʊstˈpəʊn] *vt.* 使延期，延缓；把……放在次要地位；把……放在后面
　　　　　　　　 vi. 延缓；延缓发作
congestion [kənˈdʒestʃən] *n.* 拥挤，堵车；阻塞；充血；(人口)过剩，稠密
clearance [ˈklɪrəns] *n.* 清洁，清扫；空隙，间隙；(飞机起降的)许可，准许
line up 排成一行；排队等候
extend [ɪksˈtend] *vt.* 伸展；给予；扩大
　　　　　　　　 vi. 伸出；(空间、时间等)延伸；(在长度、面积、范围等方面)扩大
ground staff 地面人员
runway [ˈrʌnweɪ] *n.* 跑道；河床；滑道
first class passengers 头等舱的乘客
main cabin 客舱
clog [klɔɡ] *vt. & vi.* 阻碍；堵塞

7.3 Before Disembarkation(下机前)

7.3.1 Water Supply System Failure(供水系统故障停止供应热饮)

Ladies and gentlemen,
Due to the water supply system failure, we will be unable to offer hot drinks on today's flight. We apologize for this inconvenience.
Thank you for your understanding.

女士们，先生们：
本架飞机由于供水系统突发故障，我们无法为您提供热饮。由此给您带来的不便，我们深表歉意。

感谢您的理解与配合！

7.3.2　Lost and Found(失物认领)

> Ladies and gentlemen,
> Which passengers are missing items in _____? Please let us know.
> Thank you!

> 女士们，先生们：
> 哪位旅客在_____丢失了物品？请与乘务员联系。
> 谢谢！

7.3.3　Request for Medical Assistance(找医生)

> Ladies and gentlemen,
> Your attention, please. We urgently need the assistance of a doctor or nurse. If there are any medical professionals on board, please approach one of the flight attendants as soon as possible.
> Thank you for your help!

> 女士们，先生们：
> 请注意，我们急需医生或护士的帮助，如果飞机上有哪位旅客是医护人士，请您尽快与乘务员联系。
> 非常感谢您的帮助！

7.3.4　Suspension of Hot Drink Service Due to Turbulence (因颠簸，暂停提供热饮)

> Ladies and gentlemen,
> We are currently experiencing some turbulence. For your safety, please return to your seat and fasten seat belt. Hot drink service will be suspended during the time.
> Thank you for your understanding!

> 女士们，先生们：
> 由于飞机遇有不稳定气流，为了您的安全，请您回原位坐好，系好安全带。在此期间我们将暂停提供热饮。
> 感谢您的理解！

7.3.5 Turbulence (Suspension of Cabin Service)[颠簸(暂停服务)]

Ladies and gentlemen,

We are currently experiencing some turbulence(climbing/descending). For your safety, please return to your seat and fasten seat belt. Refrain from using the lavatories until the sign goes off. Cabin service will be suspended during the time.

Thank you for your understanding!

女士们，先生们：

受气流影响，飞机颠簸(攀升/下降)。为了您的安全，请您立即回原位坐好，保持您的安全带紧扣。在此期间，卫生间暂停使用，客舱服务将顺延一段时间。

谢谢您的理解！

7.3.6 Headsets Collection(回收耳机)

Ladies and gentlemen,

Our aircraft is going to land at _____ airport. Our in-flight entertainment programs have now concluded. Please pass headsets to our flight attendants for collection.

Thank you for your cooperation!

女士们，先生们：

我们的飞机马上就要到达_____机场。我们的娱乐节目即将结束。乘务员将到您的面前收取耳机，请您给予协助。

谢谢您的合作！

7.3.7 Flying Directly(直飞)

Ladies and gentlemen,

We have been informed that we have to fly directly to _____ airport due to unfavorable weather conditions in (on our route to) _____. We will be landing in about _____ hours/minutes. If you need any assistance, please let us know.

Thank you!

女士们，先生们：

我们刚刚收到通知，由于_____天气状况不符合降落标准(机场关闭)，为了所有旅客的安全，我们决定直飞_____机场。预计将在_____小时/分钟后到达。如果您需要帮助请与客舱乘务员联系，我们将竭诚为您服务。

谢谢！

7.3.8　Circling(空中盘旋)

Ladies and gentlemen,

Due to the unfavorable weather conditions and poor visibility at _____ airport, we are ordered to circle over the airport until we receive new instructions.

Thank you for your understanding and cooperation!

女士们，先生们：

由于_____机场天气不好，能见度不符合降落标准，飞机暂时无法降落，我们需要在机场上空盘旋等待。进一步的消息，我们将及时通知您。

谢谢您的理解与配合！

7.3.9　Landing Delay(着陆延迟)

Ladies and gentlemen,

We've been informed that, due to _____, the aircraft will be landing in about _____ hours/minutes.

Thank you for you understanding and cooperation!

女士们，先生们：

我们刚刚收到通知，由于_____，飞机暂时无法降落，我们预计在_____小时/分钟后到达。

感谢您的理解与配合！

7.3.10　Landing in Advance(提前着陆)

Ladies and gentlemen,

We have been informed that due to strong tailwind, (under the requirements of Air Traffic Control Department) the aircraft will be landing in about _____ minutes. Please make sure your seat belt fastened.

Thank you!

女士们，先生们：

由于下降期间飞机遇有强顺风，(根据空中管制部门要求)我们将在_____分钟之后降落，请您再次确认系好安全带。

谢谢！

7.3.11 Return/Alternate Flight(返航/备降)

Ladies and gentlemen,

We have been informed that, due to _____, we can not continue to go for the safety of all passengers. We decided to return/drop/alternate in _____ airport. We are expected to arrive in _____ hours/minutes. We will keep you informed.

Thank you for your understanding and cooperation.

Reasons:
1. Bad weather in _____/over the flight route;
2. Technical problem;
3. Strike in _____ airport;
4. Sick passenger aboard aircraft.

女士们，先生们：

我们刚刚收到通知，由于_____(原因)，我们不能继续前往_____。为了所有旅客的安全，现决定返航/备降/加降_____机场。预计在_____小时/分钟后到达。进一步的消息，我们会及时通知您。

感谢您的理解与配合！

原因：
1. _____天气状况不佳/航路天气状况不好；
2. 机械故障；
3. _____机场罢工；
4. 机上有重病旅客，需紧急医疗协助。

7.3.12 Returning to Airports/Arriving in Alternate Airports (到达返航/备降机场)

Ladies and gentlemen,

We have just returned to _____ airport/arrived in the alternate airport in _____. Our plane is taxiing on the runway. Please remain seated with seat belt fastened and luggage stowed. The use of mobile phone is prohibited until the seat belt sign is switched off. Our captain is contacting the relevant department. We will keep you informed.

Thank you for your understanding!

女士们，先生们：

我们已经返航_____机场/到达_____备降机场。飞机还将滑行一段距离。请您系好安全带，把行李放好。在此期间请不要打开手机。飞机完全停稳后，机组将与相关部门联系后续事宜，请您在座位上耐心等候。进一步的消息，我们会随时广播通知您。

感谢您的理解！

7.3.13　PAX May Leave Belongings on Board(行李不拿下飞机)

Ladies and gentlemen,
Passengers continuing on to _____, you will be required to leave the aircraft and proceed to the transit lounge. Personal belongings may be left on board. But we recommend that you take valuables with you. Please obtain a boarding pass from the ground staff. We will be staying here for about _____ hour(s).
Thank you!

女士们，先生们：
继续前往_____的旅客，请您将整理好的全部手提物品放在行李架上，贵重物品请随身携带，登机牌请从地面工作人员处获取。我们的飞机将在这里停留_____小时。

谢谢！

7.3.14　Taxiing After Landing(着陆后滑行)

Ladies and gentlemen,
Our plane has just landed at _____ airport.
Our plane is taxiing along the runway. For your safety, please remain in your seat with your seat belt fastened and luggage stowed. Until the seat belt sign is switched off.
Thank you for your understanding and cooperation.

女士们，先生们：
我们的飞机已安全到达_____机场。

飞机还将滑行一段时间。为了您的安全，在安全带指示灯熄灭前请不要解开安全带去拿取行李，以免摔伤或行李砸伤其他旅客。

感谢您的理解与配合！

7.3.15　Delay (Parking Area)[等待(停机位)]

Ladies and gentlemen,
Due to the congestion at the airport, we will be making a brief stop to wait for a parking bay. Please remain in your seat and fasten your seat belt until further notice.
Thank you!

女士们，先生们：
我们刚刚接到通知，由于机场繁忙，我们的飞机需在此等待停机位，稍后还将继续滑行。请您不要解开安全带，等候进一步的通知。

谢谢！

7.3.16 Tail Support(货物太重加支尾撑杆)

Ladies and gentlemen,

Due to heavy loading, tail support must be installed before opening the door. Please remain seated until further notice.

Thank you!

女士们，先生们：

由于货物太重，本架飞机须加支尾撑杆，才能开门。请各位旅客在座位上休息，等候进一步的通知。

谢谢！

7.3.17 Delay (Transit Bus)[等待(摆渡车)]

Ladies and gentlemen,

Because of the air traffic volumn, we are waiting for the air steps(air bridge/transit bus). For your safety, please remain seated for further information.

Thank you!

女士们，先生们：

由于机场繁忙，我们的飞机需在此等待客梯(廊桥/摆渡车)到达，请您在座位上稍候片刻。

谢谢！

7.3.18 Taking the Transit Bus(停靠远机位，乘坐摆渡车)

Ladies and gentlemen,

Since our aircraft is at a bay far away from the terminal, all passengers will take the transit bus to the terminal. As the outside temperature is relatively high/low, we advise you to take off/put on your clothing when you disembark.

It is raining/snowing outside and the ground is slippery, so please watch your steps.

Thank you!

女士们，先生们：

由于我们的飞机停靠在远机位，您需要乘坐摆渡车前往候机楼。由于机舱外温度较高/低，请您在下机前适当减少/增加衣服。

雨天/雪天路滑，下机时，请小心台阶，注意脚下。

谢谢！

7.3.19　Waiting for Inspecting Officer(联检单位未到)

Ladies and gentlemen,

We have to wait for the officers of the customs, the immigration and the quarantine for inspection. Please be seated for a moment.

Thank you.

女士们，先生们：

由于海关、检疫、边防官员未到，所有旅客暂时不能下机，请您在座位上休息等候。

谢谢！

7.3.20　Announcement of Disembarkation(下机通告)

Ladies and gentlemen,

Our plane has come to a complete stop. Please take all your belongings and disembark from the front(back) door. We hope you will enjoy your stay in _____.

Thank you!

女士们，先生们：

我们的飞机已经停稳，请带好您的全部手提物品从前(后)登机门下飞机。

祝您在_____愉快！

谢谢！

7.3.21　Prompting of Getting Passports Ready for Check (提示乘客持护照下机接受检查)

Ladies and gentlemen,

According to the regulations of _____ (country/region) immigration, please get your passport ready for check by immigration officials when you get off the aircraft.

Thank you!

女士们，先生们：

根据_____(国家/地区)移民局要求，请您在下机时准备好护照，以备移民局官员在机门口检查。

谢谢！

7.3.22 Reporting a Theft Case to the Security Authorities(偷盗报案)

Ladies and gentlemen,

At the request of a passenger, we have contacted the police. Please remain in your seat after the aircraft lands and wait until the police come.

Thank you for your understanding and cooperation!

女士们，先生们：

应一位乘客要求，我们已向警方报案。请您在飞机落地后在座位坐好，等待警方到来。

感谢您的理解与配合！

Words and Expressions

water supply system 给水系统，供水系统

medical [ˈmedɪkəl] *adj.* 医学的；医疗的

approach [əˈprəʊtʃ] *vt. & vi.* 接近，走近，靠近

turbulence [ˈtɜːbjʊləns] *n.* 湍流；动荡

currently [ˈkʌrəntli] *adv.* 当前，目前

descend [dɪˈsend] *vt.* 下来；下降

unfavorable [ʌnˈfeɪvərəbəl] *adj.* 不顺利的；令人不快的；不吉利的

visibility [ˌvɪzəˈbɪlɪti] *n.* 能见度；关注程度

circle over 在……上空盘旋

tailwind [ˈteɪlwɪnd] *n.* (从后面吹来的)顺风

alternate [ɔːlˈtɜːnɪt] *adj.* 轮流的；交替的；间隔的；可代替的

tail support 支尾撑杆

install [ɪnˈstɔl] *vt.* 安装；安顿

air steps 机载客梯

air bridge 廊桥

transit bus 摆渡车

slippery [ˈslɪpəri] *adj.* 狡猾的；滑溜的；不可靠的

authority [əˈθɒrɪti] *n.* 权威人士；职权；[复数]当权者

Practice

Ⅰ. Look and Say

Guess the words or expressions of the given pictures, both in English and in Chinese.

1

2

3

4

Announcements Part III

5 6

7

8

Ⅱ. Word Matching

Match the technical terms in Column A with their definitions in Column B.

1

Column A

anniversary
postpone
adjust
decrease
auxiliary
failure
rear
congest
temporary
merge

Column B

(1) the annually recurring date of a past event, especially one of historical, national, or personal importance (周年纪念，周年纪念日：以往事件的日期每年度地重复，尤指历史、国家或个人的重要日期)

(2) to combine or unite (使合并或结合)

(3) lasting or intended to last or be used only for a limited time (暂时的：在有限的时间内持续、被使用)

(4) to change so as to match or fit; to ged used to a new situation by changing (调节，调整：改变……以相适或适应；适应)

(5) giving assistance or support (辅助的：给予帮助或支持的)

(6) the condition or fact of not achieving the desired end (失败：没有达到希望目标的状况或事实)

(7) to become or make sth become smaller in number, amount, or intensity (减少：在数目、数量或强度方面逐渐变少或使……变得少或小)

(8) to delay until a future time; put off (延迟)

(9) to overfill or overcrowd (堵塞：充满或过于拥挤)

(10) a hind part (后面，后边)

2

Column A

visibility
alternate
suspend
descend
authority
approach
medical
unfavorable
slippery
install

Column B

(1) related to illness and injury and their treatment (疾病的；医学的；医疗的)

(2) to come near or nearer in space or time(接近：在空间或时间上靠得更近)

(3) to stop for a period; interrupt(暂停一段时期；中断)

(4) to move from a higher place to a lower place; come or go down(下来：从较高的地方移到较低的地方；降下)

(5) likely to be a hindrance; disadvantageous(不顺利的；不利的)

(6) the fact, state, or degree of being visible(可见性，清晰程度：能看见的事实、状态和程度)

(7) happening or following in turns; succeeding each other continuously(轮流的，交替发生的：按顺序发生或跟随；彼此连续接替)

(8) to set in position and connect or adjust for use(安装：放入其位置并安装连接好或调整以供使用)

(9) causing or tending to cause sliding or slipping(滑溜的：能引起或倾向于引起打滑或滑倒的)

(10) the power to enforce laws, exact obedience, command, determine, or judge(权力：能够执行法律、规章、命令、决定或判决的力量)

III. Announcement Completion

Fill in the blanks with words or expressions given, and then work in pairs to read aloud to each other.

Announcement 1

| beverages | due | failure | conditioning | cooperation |
| properly | details | auxiliary | inform | equipment |

Ladies and gentlemen,

We are sorry to ___(1)___ you that ___(2)___ to the ___(3)___ power supply ___(4)___, air ___(5)___ does not function ___(6)___ on the ground. We have already informed the relevant departments for ground support ___(7)___, and cabin temperature will gradually decrease. We will provide you with more ___(8)___ as soon as they become available. We will now offer ___(9)___.

Thank you for your understanding and ___(10)___.

Announcement 2

| aircraft | bay | terminal | transit | relatively | steps |

Ladies and gentlemen,

Since our ___(1)___ is at a ___(2)___ far away from the ___(3)___, all passengers will take the ___(4)___ bus to the terminal. As the outside temperature is ___(5)___ high, we advise you to take off your clothing when you disembark.

It is raining outside and the ground is slippery, so please watch your ___(6)___.

Thank you!

IV. Individual Work

Read the announcements for special occasions in this unit loudly, and pay attention to both pronunciation and intonation.

Ⅴ. Further Study

1. 免税店

免税店指经海关总署批准，由经营单位在中华人民共和国国务院或其授权部门批准的地点设立符合海关监管要求的销售场所和存放免税品的监管仓库，向规定的对象销售、供应免税品的商店。目前，我国境内的免税店主要有口岸免税店、运输工具免税店、市内免税店、外交人员免税店、供船免税店及我国出国人员外汇免税商店。

免税运进专供是指免税店向规定的对象销售、供应的进口商品。免税店经营的免税品种，应由经营单位统一报经海关总署批准。免税店销售的免税进口烟草制品和酒精饮料在其内、外包装的显著位置上加印"中国关税未付"(China Duty Not Paid)的中、英文字样。

各国家免税店的购物方式不太一样，比如在韩国免税店购物，需要提供护照和回程机票，买的东西如果是韩国品牌则可以带走，如果是外国品牌则不能带走，需要回程时在机场提货，且有金额限制。而在日本只要出示护照和机票就可以直接购买免税品。香港免税店实际上不是真正意义上的免税店，因为香港本身就是自由港，没有关税，所以不需要任何手续。而在欧洲消费者可以在任何商店购买商品，然后只需凭借其购买发票到机场退税就可以了。

2. 机场摆渡车

由于现在的机场飞机数量多，机位少，而建设一个机位所需要的资金又很大，所以差不多有三分之二的飞机降落后停留在了远机位。为了保障乘客下飞机后能安全、快速地从远机位到机场出口，这就需要通过机场摆渡车来运送乘客。乘客每次在摆渡车内耽搁的时间有 12 分钟左右。摆渡车在机场 24 小时运转，每天要工作 72 个来回。

Unit 8　　Emergency Announcements

8.1　Fire in the Cabin(客舱失火)

8.1.1　Decompression(客舱释压)

Ladies and gentlemen,

Attention, please, sit down immediately. Pull an oxygen mask firmly toward yourself. Place the mask over your nose and mouth and breathe normally.

Put on your own mask first before assisting others.

Please remain seated with your seat belt fastened until further instructed.

女士们，先生们：

请乘客们立即就坐。请用力拉下面罩，罩在口鼻处进行正常呼吸。

戴好自己的氧气罩后再去帮助别人。

请大家在下一个指令发布前，在自己的座位上坐好，系好安全带。

8.1.2　Announcement of the Cabin Fire(客舱失火通告)

Ladies and gentlemen,

We are putting out a minor fire that has broken out in the lavatory in the front/center/rear of the cabin. Passengers sitting in the front/center/rear, please follow the cabin attendants' directions. All other passengers please do not leave your seats.

女士们，先生们：

现在飞机前/中/后舱卫生间失火，我们正在组织灭火，坐在火源附近的旅客，请听从乘务员指挥。其他旅客请您坐好，不要离开座位。

8.1.3　Fire Extinguished(灭火后)

Ladies and gentlemen,

The fire has been completely put out. The plane is cruising as scheduled to _____. Thank you for your assistance and cooperation.

Thank you!

女士们，先生们：

火已被完全扑灭。飞机处于良好状态，我们将继续飞往_____。非常感谢您的协助和合作。

谢谢！

8.1.4　Emergency Landing (Ditching)[陆地(海上)迫降]

Ladies and gentlemen,

Attention, please. This is the chief purser. We are forced to make an emergency landing (ditching). The crew has been well trained to handle this type of situation. We assure you that you'll be safe with us. Please be seated and keep calm. And follow the flight attendants' directions.

女士们，先生们：

请注意，您好，我是本次航班的乘务长。我们决定采取陆地(海上)迫降。对于处理这种情况，我们全体机组人员都受过良好的训练。我们有信心、有能力保证您的安全。请您回座位坐好，保持安定，注意听从乘务员的指挥。

8.1.5　Emergency Announcements(On Behalf of the Captain) [紧急广播(代表机长)]

Ladies and gentlemen,

This is the chief purser. The captain has advised us that we are making an immediate emergency landing in _____ minutes. Please keep calm and remain in your seat until further instructed.

女士们，先生们：

您好，我是本次航班的乘务长。根据机长指示我们将在_____分钟后紧急着陆。现在请您保持安定，坐好，并听从乘务员指挥。

Words and Expressions

decompression [ˌdiːkəmˈpreʃən] *n.* 减压，解压；泄压
breathe [briːð] *vi.* 呼吸
normally [ˈnɔːməlɪ] *adv.* 正常地；通常地，一般地；按常规的
assist [əˈsɪst] *vt.* 帮助；援助；帮助某人做某事
instruct [ɪnˈstrʌkt] *vt.* 教；教导，指导；指示；吩咐
put out 扑灭；关闭
minor [ˈmaɪnə] *adj.* 次要的；不严重的；小调的
direction [dɪˈrekʃən] *n.* 方向；指引，指示；用法说明
follow directions 听从指挥
extinguish [ɪkˈstɪŋgwɪʃ] *vt.* 熄灭(火)
make an emergency landing 紧急着陆
ditch [dɪtʃ] *vi.* 使(飞机)在海上紧急降落，(在海上)迫降
purser [ˈpɜːsə] *n.* 乘务长

8.2 Announcements by the Crew Chief(乘务长广播)

8.2.1 Cabin Tidying and Seatback/Table Fastening (客舱整理、固定好座椅靠背/小桌板)

Ladies and gentlemen,

Please get all your tray sets and other service items ready for passing to the cabin attendants.

Place your seatback and table to the upright position, stow footrest and in-seat video units, and keep your seat belt fastened.

女士们，先生们：

请将您的餐盘和其他服务用具准备好，以便乘务员收取。

请调直座椅靠背，固定好小桌板，收起脚踏板和座位上的录像装置，并系好安全带。

8.2.2　Introduction to the Exit(紧急出口介绍)

Ladies and gentlemen,

The emergency lights on the floor will direct you to the exit. White lights mark the escape path and the red ones, the exits. Please locate at least two of the exits.

When evacuating, please leave the aircraft by the nearest exit and do not take any baggage.

Inflate your life vest at the exit.

女士们，先生们：

地板上的应急撤离路线灯将把您引导到出口处。白色为撤离路线灯，红色为出口指示灯。请确认至少两个以上的出口。

应急撤离时，请从最近的出口撤离，不要携带任何物品。

在到达出口时，请给您的救生衣充气。

8.2.3　Aid Donors Selection(选择援助者)

Ladies and gentlemen,

If you are airlines staff, fire fighter or soldier, please let us know. We need your help.

女士们，先生们：

如果您是航空公司的雇员、消防人员或军人，请与乘务员联系。我们需要您的协助。

8.2.4　Taking Away Sharp Objects(取下尖锐物品)

Ladies and gentlemen,

For your safety during the evacuation, please take away sharp objects such as pens, barrette, knives, watches and jewelries items, untie things like ties and scarves, take off high-heeled shoes and put them all into your luggage. Eyeglasses, denture and deaf-aid should be put into your coat pocket.

The seat pocket in front of you should be kept empty. Please stow all your baggage in the overhead compartment or under your seat.

女士们，先生们：

疏散时为了您的安全，请取下随身的尖硬物品，如钢笔、发夹、小刀、手表和首饰，解下领带和围巾，脱下带跟鞋，把这些物品放入行李里。眼镜、假牙和助听器放在上衣口袋内。

请不要把任何东西放在您前面的座椅口袋里。所有行李请放在座位底下或行李架内。

8.2.5 Safety Position(防冲击姿势说明)

Ladies and gentlemen,
Now, the cabin attendant will show you two kinds of safety positions.

First, keep the upper part of your body upright and strained, grasp the arms of your seat with your two hands firmly, and place both your feet firmly on the floor.

Second, stretch both your arms and cross them on the seatback in front of you, lower your head and place both your feet firmly on the floor.

Take one of these positions when you hear "brace!" until you hear "unfasten seat belt!"

During emergency landing (ditching), there will be a few impacts. Take your brace position until the aircraft comes to a complete stop.

女士们，先生们：
为了您的安全，现在乘务员将向您介绍两种防冲击姿势。

第1种：上身挺直，收紧下颌，双手用力抓住座椅扶手，两脚用力蹬地。

第2种：两臂伸直交叉，紧抓前方座椅靠背，头俯下，两脚用力蹬地。

当您听到"低头弯腰，紧迫用力！"的口令时采取任意一种姿势，直到您听到"解开安全带"的口令为止。

飞机紧急着陆时，会有多次撞击，保持这种姿势直到飞机完全停稳。

8.2.6 Demonstration of the Usage of a Life Vest (救生衣使用演示)

Ladies and gentlemen,
Now, the cabin attendant will demonstrate how to use life vest. Please put on your life vest as directed, but do not inflate them in the cabin.

The life vest is under your seat. Take it out and unwrap it, slip it on over your head. Fasten the buckles and pull tightly.

When you leave the aircraft, pull the red tab to inflate. Please do not inflate it while in the cabin.

If your vest needs further inflation, you can pull out the two mouthpieces in the upper part of the vest and blow into them.

(At night) At last, please pull off the seal of battery.

女士们，先生们：
现在乘务员将向您演示救生衣的使用方法，请旅客们随同乘务员的演示穿上救生衣，但请不要在客舱内充气。

救生衣在您座位底下，取出并撕开包装，将救生衣经头部穿好，将带子扣好，系紧。

当您离开飞机时，拉下救生衣两侧的红色充气把手，但在客舱内请不要充气。

充气不足时，可将救生衣上部的人工充气管拉出，用嘴向里吹气。

(在夜间)最后拔掉电池销。

8.2.7　Safety Instructions Leaflet(安全说明书)

Ladies and gentlemen,

The safety instructions leaflet are in the seat pocket in front of you, please read them carefully. If you have any questions, please ask your neighbour or cabin attendant.

女士们，先生们：

在您前方座椅口袋里有安全说明书，请仔细阅读。如果您有疑问请向邻座旅客或乘务员询问。

8.2.8　Security Tips(安全提示)

1

Ladies and gentlemen,

You will take brace position for impact when you are given the command "brace". Keep brace position until the aircraft comes to a complete stop. Then unfasten your seat belt and evacuate from the exits as directed by the flight attendants. Don't take any baggage in evacuation.

(Evacuation on water) Inflate your life vest at the exit.

2

Ladies and gentlemen,

Please remove eyeglasses, denture and deaf-aid, and put them in your coat pocket.

1

女士们，先生们：

当乘务员发出"全身紧迫用力"的命令时，您要做好防冲击姿势，并保持防冲击姿势直到飞机完全停稳。然后解开安全带，听从客舱乘务员的指挥进行应急撤离。应急撤离时，不要携带任何物品。

(水上撤离)在到达出口时，打开救生衣的充气阀门。

2

女士们，先生们：

现在请拿下眼镜、假牙和助听器，并将它们放在外衣口袋内。

8.2.9 Cabin Lights Dimming(调暗客舱灯光)

Ladies and gentlemen,
Now we will dim the cabin lights to help you to fit in with the darkness outside.

女士们,先生们:
为了使您的眼睛能尽快适应外部光线,我们将调暗客舱灯光。

8.2.10 Upper Deck Exits Boeing 747(B747 飞机上舱紧急出口)

Ladies and gentlemen,
For passengers seated in the upper deck, may I have your attention, please. Your emergency exits are located in the main cabin downstairs. In addition, there are two alternative exits upstairs. Please follow the attendants' instru-ction when evacuating.

女士们,先生们:
坐在上舱的旅客请注意,您的应急出口在楼下左右侧,上舱还有两个备用应急出口。撤离时,请听从指挥。

8.2.11 Before Emergency Landing(着陆前防冲击警告广播)

Ladies and gentlemen,
Attention please. It is now time for emergency landing (ditching).
Brace for impact!

女士们,先生们:
请注意,飞机马上紧急着陆。

请立即做好安全姿势。

Words and Expressions

tidy [ˈtaɪdɪ] *adj.* 整洁的,整齐的
　　　　　 vt. & vi. 使整洁;弄整齐;整理
emergency light　紧急照明灯,事故照明器
mark [mɑːk] *vt.* 做记号;表明

escape path　疏散通道

exit [ˈeksɪt] *n.* 出口，通道

evacuation [ɪˌvækjuˈeɪʃən] *n.* 撤空；撤离；撤退；疏散

barrette [bəˈret] *n.* (妇女用的)条状发夹

jewelry [ˈdʒuəlrɪ] *n.* 珠宝，首饰

untie [ʌnˈtaɪ] *vi.* 松开，解开

scarf [skɑ:f] *n.* 围巾

heel [hi:l] *n.* 脚后跟；鞋后跟

denture [ˈdentʃə] *n.* (一副)假牙；托牙

deaf-aid [ˈdefeɪd] *n.* 助听器

unwrap [ʌnˈræp] *vt.* 打开；拆开

brace [breɪs] *vt.* 支撑；准备；绷紧
　　　　　　 vi. 准备好

fire fighter　救火队员

Practice

Ⅰ. Look and Say

Guess the meaning of the given pictures, both in English and in Chinese.

1

2

Announcements Part III

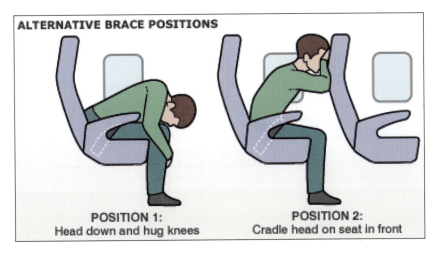

3

4

Ⅱ. Word Matching

Match the technical terms in Column A with their definitions in Column B.

Column A

- minor
- evacuation
- cruise
- normal
- direction
- extinguish
- instruct
- ditch
- unwrap
- untie

Column B

(1) to crash-land in the sea; used by an aircraft or a pilot(在海上迫降；用于飞机或驾驶员)

(2) to put out a fire; quench(熄灭；扑灭)

(3) to sail or travel about, as for pleasure or reconnaissance(巡游，航行，航游：为娱乐或侦察而进行航行或巡航)

(4) the act or function of directing(指导，指挥：指导的动作或作用)

(5) to provide with knowledge, especially in a methodical way(教授；提供知识)

(6) conforming with, adhering to, or constituting a norm, standard, pattern, level, or type; typical(正常的：符合、遵循或构成一个准则、标准、方式、水平或形式的；典型的)

(7) to remove the wrapping or wrappings from or become unwrapped(拿下打开：把包裹物从……上面拿下或被打开)

(8) to undo or loosen(解开或松开)

(9) the act of evacuating or the condition of being evacuated(撤离的行为或被撤离的状态)

(10) lesser or smaller in amount, extent, or size(较小的，较少的：在数量、规模或尺寸上较少或较小的)

Announcements Part III

III. Announcement Completion

Fill in the blanks with words or expressions given, and then work in pairs to read aloud to each other.

Announcement 1

| before | with | toward | on | normally |
| over | remain | until | immediately | firmly |

Ladies and gentlemen,

Attention, please, sit down __(1)__. Pull an oxygen mask firmly __(2)__ __(3)__ yourself. Place the mask __(4)__ your nose and mouth and breathe __(5)__. Put __(6)__ your own mask first __(7)__ assisting others. Please __(8)__ seated __(9)__ your seat belt fastened __(10)__ further instructed.

Announcement 2

| escape | white | exits | nearest | locate |
| exit | direct | red | evacuating | vest |

Ladies and gentlemen,

The emergency lights on the floor will __(1)__ you to the exit. __(2)__ lights mark the __(3)__ path and the __(4)__ ones, the __(5)__. Please __(6)__ at least two of the exits.

When __(7)__, please leave the aircraft by the __(8)__ exit and do not take any baggage.

Inflate your life __(9)__ at the __(10)__.

Announcement 3

| braceant | upper | strained | positions | cross |
| emergency | upright | attendant | impacts | stretch |

Ladies and gentlemen,

Now, the cabin ___(1)___ will show you two kinds of safety ___(2)___.

First, keep the ___(3)___ part of your body ___(4)___ and ___(5)___ grasp the arms of your seat with your two hands firmly, and place both your feet firmly on the floor.

Second, ___(6)___ both your arms and ___(7)___ them on the seatback in front of you, lower your head and place both your feet firmly on the floor.

Take one of these positions when you hear "___(8)___!" until you hear "unfasten seat belt!"

During ___(9)___ landing, there will be a few ___(10)___. Take your brace position until the aircraft comes to a complete stop.

Ⅳ. Individual Work

Read the announcements for emergency in this unit loudly, and pay attention to both pronunciation and intonation.

Ⅴ. Further Study

Read the following paragraph and then answer the questions below.

Questions: What is the function of brace position? How do we instruct passengers to practice it?

Take Brace Position

It has been proven that passengers who assume the brace position sustain substantially less serious injuries than other passengers. A twin engined aircraft struck terrain during a landing approach in less than favorable conditions. Most of the 16 passengers were sleeping or reading and there was no warning of the imminent accident. One passenger woke up, looked out the window and saw the aircraft was about to hit trees. He immediately lowered his head and braced his arms and knees against the seatback in front of him. He suffered a fractured leg and wrist and a scalp wound. He was the only survivor.

Note

1. substantially [səbˈstænʃəlɪ] *adv.* 本质上，实质上；很大程度地

    The price was substantially higher than had been expected. 价格比预计的要高很多。

2. terrain [təˈren] *n.* 地形，地势；地面，地带

    The terrain changed quickly from arable land to desert. 那个地带很快就从耕地变成了

沙漠。

3. imminent [ˈɪmɪnənt] *adj.* (通常指不愉快的事)即将发生的

There appeared no imminent danger. 眼前似乎没有危险。

4. fracture [ˈfræktʃə] *vt.* & *vi.* (使)折断，分裂

　　　　　　　n. 断裂；骨折

He suffered a fractured skull. 他的头骨开裂了。

5. scalp [skælp] *n.* 头皮

He was rubbing his sore scalp. 他正揉着发痛的头皮。

Unit 9　　Airport Announcements(机场广播)

9.1　Paging Departure(登机广播)

Attention, please!

China Eastern Airlines announces the departure of Flight MU535 to Hong Kong. Will passengers for this flight please proceed to Gate 10?

Thank you!

旅客们请注意：

飞往香港的东航 MU535 次航班，现在开始登机了。请该航班的旅客到 10 号门去登机。

谢谢！

9.2　Commencement of Check-in(办理登机手续广播)

Good morning (afternoon/evening), ladies and gentlemen,

Air China Flight CA 981 to New York is now ready for check-in. Passengers on that flight please have your baggage and tickets ready and proceed to Air China Counter 14.

Thank you!

女士们，先生们，早上(下午/晚上)好：

飞往纽约的国航 CA981 次航班，现在开始办理登机手续。请旅客们拿好行李和机票，到国航 14 号柜台办理。

谢谢！

9.3　Check-in Closing(登机手续即将完毕广播)

1

Check-in for Air China Flight CA981 bound for New York will be closed in a few minutes. Passengers who have not yet checked in please come to Air China counter.

Thank you!

1

飞往纽约的国航 CA981 次航班，即将办完登机手续。还未办理的旅客，请到国航柜台办理。

谢谢！

Announcements Part III

2

Attention, please, passengers to New York:

Air China Flight 981 is now closing. Passengers for this flight who have not yet checked in should do so now at Counter 14.

2

前往纽约去的旅客请注意：

国航 981 次航班，即将停止办理登机手续。还未办理登机的旅客，请到十四号柜台办理。

9.4 Commencement of Boarding(开始登机广播)

1

Attention, please. Passengers bound for Los Angeles on Flight MU583, your flight will be boarding in 15 minutes. In order to speed up boarding, please have your tickets ready.

Thank you!

2

Thank you for waiting, ladies and gentlemen. Flight CA985 for San Francisco is now ready for boarding. Passengers on this flight please make your way to Gate 15. Please refrain from smoking beyond the gate.

Thank you!

3

Your attention, please. Fight CA1603 for Harbin is boarding now at Gate No.5.

Thank you!

1

乘坐飞往洛杉矶的 MU583 次航班的旅客请注意：您乘坐的航班 15 分钟后开始登机。为了尽快登机，请准备好您的机票。

谢谢！

2

女士们，先生们，感谢您在此恭候。前往旧金山的 CA985 次航班，现已开始登机。请乘坐该航班的旅客到 15 号门登机。出门登机请勿吸烟！

谢谢！

3

旅客们请注意：中国国际航空公司前往哈尔滨的 CA1603 次航班，现已在 5 号门登机。

谢谢！

9.5　Final Boarding Call(登机最后一次广播)

1

Attention, please. This is the final call for passengers traveling to Tokyo. Flight CA951 is now boarding. Passengers are kindly requested to proceed to Gate 20.

2

This is the final boarding call for passengers departing on Flight MU515 for Osaka. Please passengers on this flight go immediately to Gate 15.

3

This is the last call for China Eastern Airlines Flight MU535 for Hong Kong. All passengers board at Gate 2.

1

前往东京去的旅客请注意，这是登机的最后广播。CA951 次航班现已登机，请旅客们前往 20 号门登机。

2

乘坐 MU515 次航班前往大阪的旅客，这是登机的最后广播。请该航班的旅客马上到 15 号门登机。

3

这是登机的最后广播。中国东方航空公司 MU535 次航班飞往香港的全体旅客，请到 2 号门去登机。

9.6　Boarding Announcement for Delayed Departure (航班延误后的登机广播)

Thank you for waiting, ladies and gentlemen. The maintenance of the aircraft has been completed. Air China Flight CA985 to San Francisco is now ready for boarding through Gate 9.

Thank you.

女士们，先生们，谢谢在此等候。飞机维修现已结束。国航飞往旧金山的 CA985 次航班，现已在 9 号门开始登机。

谢谢。

Announcements Part III

9.7 Irregularity Delay Due to Weather Indefinite Time
(因天气原因，航班非正常延误广播)

May I have your attention, please? Air China regrets to announce that the departure of Flight CA957 to Singapore will be delayed due to unfavorable weather conditions in Singapore. We are monitoring weather reports and will keep you informed. You are kindly requested to wait in this lounge until further notice.

Thank you!

旅客们请注意，中国国际航空公司抱歉地通知各位，由于新加坡的天气原因，飞往新加坡的 CA957 次航班将延误起飞。我们正关注天气预报的变化，并与各位保持联系。请旅客们在候机室等候通知。

谢谢！

9.8 Irregularity Delay Due to Weather Definite Departure Time(因天气原因航班延误，起飞时间确定的广播)

May I have your attention, please? China Eastern Airlines regrets to announce that the departure of Flight MU535 to Hong Kong will be delayed due to unfavorable weather conditions in Hong Kong. The new departure time will be 11:30. We expect to begin boarding at about 11:00 o'clock.

Thank you!

各位旅客请注意，中国东方航空公司抱歉地通知各位：由于香港地区的天气原因，飞往香港的 MU535 次航班将延误起飞，新的起飞时间为 11:30。我们预期在 11:00 开始登机。

谢谢！

9.9 Refreshments Are Offered Due to Delay
(因延误而提供免费餐饮的广播)

Attention, please. China Eastern Airlines Flight MU582 to Shanghai will be delayed because of weather conditions at Hong Kong International Airport. A further announcement will be made not later than 10:30. In the meantime passengers are invited to take light refreshments with the compliments of the airlines at the buffet in this lounge.

各位旅客请注意：由于香港国际机场的天气原因，飞往上海的东航 MU582 次航班将延误起飞。何时起飞请听 10:30 之前的广播。现在请旅客们到候机室餐饮部免费享用航空公司提供的点心。

9.10 Delay Due to Maintenance
(因飞机维修，航班延误的广播)

Your attention, please. Air France regrets to announce that the departure of Flight AF285 to Paris will be delayed due to maintenance of the aircraft. New departure time will be announced at about 9:30. Passengers are requested to wait in this lounge until further notice.

Thank you!

旅客们请注意：法国航空公司很抱歉地通知各位，前往巴黎的 AF285 次航班，因飞机维修，将延误起飞。新的起飞时间约于 9:30 通知各位，请旅客们在候机室休息等候进一步通知。

谢谢！

9.11 Delay Due to Technical Reasons
(因技术原因，航班延误的广播)

Japan Airlines regrets to announce the delay in the departure of Flight JL785 to Beijing. Due to technical reasons, this flight is now expected to depart at 10:40 local time.

日本航空公司很抱歉地通知各位，前往北京的日航 JL785 次航班，将延误起飞。由于技术上的原因，预计该航班于当地时间 10:40 起飞。

Announcements

9.12 Anticipated Diversion or Return (航班预计改航或回航的广播)

May I have your attention, please? British Airways regrets to announce that due to the forecast of changeable weather conditions in the local airport Flight BA038 may have to be diverted to an alternative airport. If you have any questions, please contact BA agents.

Thank you!

旅客们请注意：英国航空公司很抱歉地通知各位，由于当地机场上的天气有变化，英航 BA038 次航班可能改航至另一机场，旅客若有问题请与英国航空公司乘务员联系。

谢谢！

9.13 Cancellations(航班取消广播)

1

May I have your attention, please? Air China regrets to announce that Flight CA1355 for Haikou will be cancelled as the local airport has been closed down due to a typhoon. Passengers for Flight 1355 please come to Air China Counter 20.

Thank you!

2

Attention, please. British Airways Flight BA564 to Zurich has been cancelled because of weather conditions at local airport in London. Passengers please collect your hand baggage and go to the rear exit of this lounge. Please have your passports ready and proceed downstairs to counter 17 where information about re-bookings, refunds and alternative transport is available.

1

旅客们请注意，中国国际航空公司抱歉地通知各位，因台风原因，海口当地机场已被关闭，前往海口的 CA1355 次航班将被取消。请该航班的旅客去国航 20 号柜台。

谢谢！

2

旅客们请注意，前往苏黎士的英国航空公司 BA564 次航班，因伦敦当地机场天气不好，现已被取消。请旅客带好自己的手提行李，前往候机室的后门出口处，并准备好各自的护照前往楼下 17 号柜台办理重新订票、退票，或换乘其他航班。

9.14 Connecting Passenger Information(联程航班广播)

Attention, please, passengers connected onto Air China Flight CA981 for New York please come to Air China connecting service counter in the satellite.

Thank you!

转乘国航 CA981 次联程航班，飞往纽约的旅客请注意，请去卫星厅的国航联程航班服务柜台。

谢谢！

9.15 Boarding Announcement(通知旅客登机广播)

Air China is paging passenger Fields departing on Flight CA981 to New York. Will passenger Fields please come to Air China counter?

Thank you!

乘坐 CA981 次航班飞往纽约的旅客菲尔兹先生请注意，请您听到中国国际航空公司广播后，去国航柜台办理登机手续。

谢谢！

9.16 Paging for Standby Passenger(通知候补旅客广播)

Attention, please. Standby passengers for China Eastern Airlines Flight MU5535 to Wenzhou please come to Counter 17.

Thank you!

乘坐东方航空公司 MU5535 次航班，飞往温州的候补旅客请注意，请到 17 号柜台。

谢谢！

9.17 Paging for Claiming Baggage(通知认领行李广播)

China Eastern Airlines is paging Mr. Jackson arriving on Flight MU584 from Los Angeles. Will Mr. Jackson please come to the information counter in the baggage claim area?

Thank you!

乘坐东航 MU584 次航班来自洛杉矶的杰克逊先生请注意，请您听到中国东方航空公司的广播后，到行李问询处。

谢谢！

Announcements Part III

9.18 Customs Clearance(办理结关手续广播)

Passengers from Tokyo on Flight JL791, attention, please. Please remain in this lounge until called for customs clearance. Passengers with hand baggage only may go through now for customs clearance.

乘坐日航 791 次航班，来自东京的旅客请注意，请在候机室等候办理结关手续的通知。携带手提行李的旅客现在可以办理结关手续。

9.19 Customs Clearance and Baggage Claim (办理结关手续并认领行李广播)

Passengers from Tokyo on Flight JL791 please go through channel No. 2 for customs clearance. After clearance baggage should be reclaimed in the baggage claim area.

乘坐日航 791 次航班，来自东京的旅客请注意，请前往第二通道办理海关手续，结关后，请到行李认领处领取各自的行李。

9.20 Bus Service Available(班车服务广播)

Bus service is available for all newly arrived passengers who need transportation. (Repeating)Bus service is available for all newly arrived passengers who need transportation.

刚进港旅客如需用车可乘坐班车出港。再通知一遍，需要用车的进港旅客可乘坐班车出港。

Words and Expressions

page [ˈpeɪdʒ] *vt.*　(在公共场合通过广播)呼叫
China Eastern Airlines　中国东方航空公司

proceed to 去往(某地)，进(转)入

check-in [tʃekɪn] n. 验票并领取登机卡；(机场的)检票口，办理登机手续处

close [kləuz] vt. 关闭

bound for 飞往；驶往

speed up (使)加速；增速

Los Angeles 洛杉矶(美国城市)

San Francisco 旧金山(美国加利福尼亚西部港市)

commencement [kəˈmensmənt] n. 开始；毕业典礼

final [ˈfaɪnəl] adj. 最后的；最终的；不可更改的

Harbin [ˈhɑ:rbin] n. 哈尔滨(黑龙江省省会)

Osaka [əuˈsɑ:kə] n. 大阪(日本本州岛西南岸港市)

maintenance [ˈmeɪntɪnəns] n. 维持，保持；赡养费；检修

irregularity [ɪˌregjʊˈlærɪtɪ] n. 不规则，无规律

indefinite [ɪnˈdefɪnɪt] adj. 不确定的；不明确的，模糊的

Singapore [ˌsɪŋəˈpɔ:] n. 新加坡(东南亚国家)

monitor [ˈmɒnɪtə] vt. 监控，监听

in the meantime 在……期间，同时；与此同时

with the compliments of 敬赠；谨赠

buffet [ˈbʌfɪt] n. 饮食柜台，(火车的)餐饮部；自助餐

changeable [ˈtʃeɪndʒəbəl] adj. 多变的；常变化的

BA agent 英国航空公司(British Airways) 服务员

cancellation [ˌkænsəˈleɪʃən] n. 取消；作废

Zurich [ˈzuərɪk] n. 苏黎世

stand by 支持；做好准备；信守诺言；袖手旁观表不满

standby passengers 候补旅客

baggage claim area 行李问询处

clearance [ˈklɪərəns] n. 清洁，清扫；官方许可

customs clearance 结关，海关放行；报关

go through (法律、合同等正式)获得通过；通读；检查；经历

repeat [rɪˈpi:t] vt. 复述；重复

transportation [ˌtrænspɔ:ˈteɪʃən] n. 运送，运输；运输系统；运输工具

Announcements Part III

Practice

Ⅰ. Look and Say

Guess the meaning of the given pictures, both in English and in Chinese.

1

2

3

Ⅱ. Word Matching

Match the technical terms in Column A with their definitions in Column B.

Column A

irregularity
transportation
compliment
changeable
maintenance
indefinite
page
commencement
standby
clearance

Column B

(1) to summon or call a person by name(通过名字唤或叫)

(2) a beginning; a start (开始；开端)

(3) the work of keeping something in proper condition; upkeep (养护：使某事物处于正常的工作状态；维修)

(4) the quality or state of being irregular (不规则性：不规则的性质或状态)

(5) not definite (不明确的)

(6) an expression of praise, admiration, or congratulation (恭维：赞美、羡慕或祝贺的表达方式)

(7) the act or an instance of transporting(运送：运输的行为或事例)

(8) permission for an aircraft, ship, or other vehicle to proceed, after an inspection of equipment or cargo or during certain traffic conditions(结关，准许通行：让飞机、轮船或其他交通运输工具继续前进的许可，经过对设备和货物的检查或在特定的交通状况下)

(9) a person or thing that can always be used if needed, for example if sb/sth else is not available or if there is an emergency (后备人员，备用物品)

(10) liable to change; capricious(很可能变化的；易变的)

III. Announcement Completion

Fill in the blanks with words or expressions given, and then work in pairs to read aloud to each other.

Announcement 1

| departure   further   delayed   announce   requested   monitoring   regrets |

May I have your attention, please? Air China __(1)__ to __(2)__ that the __(3)__ of Flight CA957 to Singapore will be __(4)__ due to unfavorable weather conditions in Singapore. We are __(5)__ weather reports and will keep you informed. You are kindly __(6)__ to wait in this lounge until __(7)__ notice.

Thank you!

Announcement 2

| cancelled   collect   rear   proceed   re-bookings   alternative |

Attention, please. British Airways Flight BA564 to Zurich has been __(1)__ because of weather conditions at local airport in London. Will passengers please __(2)__ their hand baggage and go to the __(3)__ exit of this lounge? Please have your passports ready and __(4)__ downstairs to counter 17 where information about __(5)__, refunds and __(6)__ transport is available.

IV. Individual Work

Read the airport announcements in this unit loudly, and pay attention to both pronunciation and intonation.

V. Further Study

1. 英国航空公司

英国航空（British Airways）又称不列颠航空，简称"英航"，总部设在英国伦敦希思罗机场，以伦敦希思罗机场(Heathrow Airport)作为枢纽基地。英国航空公司的历史可追溯到 1924 年成立的帝国航空，是英国历史最悠久的航空公司。英国航空公司是全球最大的国际航空客运航空公司,是全球七大货运航空公司之一。英航也是"寰宇一家"航空联盟的创始成员之一。

英航在 IATA 中的代码:BA

英航在 ICAO 中的代码:BAW

飞行重点城市:曼彻斯特国际机场

飞行常旅客奖励计划:行政会

呼号:Speedbird 英航的波音 747

2. 结关

结关(Customs Clearance)是指对经口岸放行后仍需继续实施管理的货物,海关在固定的期限内进行核查,对需要补证、补税货物做出处理直至完全结束海关监管的工作程序。

加工贸易进口货物的结关,是指海关在加工贸易合同规定的期限内对其进口、复出口及余料情况进行核对,并经经营单位申请办理了经批准内销部分的货物的补证、补税手续,对备案的加工贸易手册予以销案的工作程序。

暂时进出口货物的结关,是指在海关规定的期限内(含经批准延期的)暂时进口货物复运出口或者暂时出口货物复运进口,并办理了有关纳税销案手续,完全结束海关监管的工作程序。

特定减免税货物的结关,是指有关进口货物到达海关监管年限并向海关提出解除监管申请,领取了经主管海关核发的《海关对减免税进出口货物解除监管证明》,完全结束海关监管的工作程序。

简单地说,结关就是办结该批货物的一切海关手续。

Announcements Part III

3. Identify each department of the airport in the following maps

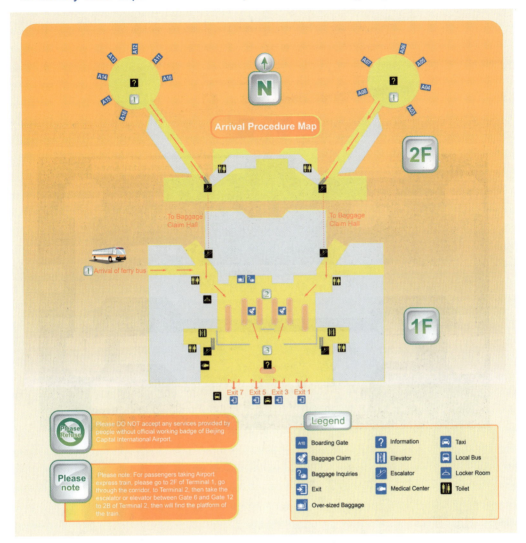

1

2

3

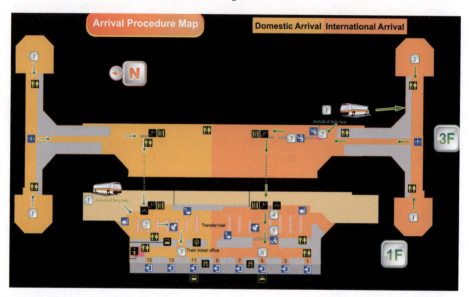

4

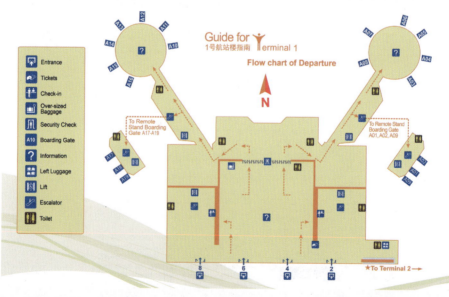

5